*Management One-Point-Oh is a full-on re
hundreds of management and leadership
take themselves too seriously, lean on the same old clichés, and
imply that leading people successfully requires complex and
elusive secrets from the High Mount. This must-read might
just keep the new manager from those pitfalls and lays out in
plain English (and humor) a road map for success.*
—Tim E. / Vice President of Operations

*In my career as a labor lawyer exclusively representing
employers, I don't recall a more straightforward and common
sense collection of principles for managers. For most any kind
of business relationship, Frazier's experience and insight
provide solid and humorous guidance for success.*
—Jonathan H. / Labor Attorney

*Management One-Point-Oh is a hilarious read on the age-old
art of people management. Frazier captures everything they
failed to tell you in college and does it in a fast, fun, spot-on
overview. Well worth the price of tuition.*
—Chuck F. / Senior V. P. of Operations

*The One Minute Manager was about "how" to manage.
Management One-Point-Oh is not only about the "how"—but
also and more importantly—the "why." It is a must read for new
managers and a good refresher course for even the most seasoned.*
—Tim C. / Former G.M. and colleague

Management One-Point-Oh

The essential characteristics of a great manager

David Samuel Frazier

Copyright © David Samuel Frazier 2019

All rights reserved. No part of this publication may be reproduced, stored in a retrieval system, or transmitted in any form or by any means, mechanical, photocopying, recording or otherwise, without prior permission in writing of the author.

ISBN: 9781078216463 (paperback)

Cover and photo: Jolanta Frazier

*To my wife Jolanta
Always.
Wiecej Niz Zycie*

*Special thanks to
Joseph Bean for his valuable insight and edits
And
Joanna Awai for her ability to catch the mistakes we didn't*

Contents

Acknowledgements xi
Forward.. xiii

1.01 How? 1
1.02 Humility 5
1.03 It's Not About The Money... 14
1.04 It's Your Fault 18
1.05 The Customer 24
1.06 Bad Managers.. 39
1.07 Glass Houses 42
1.08 Sex 47
1.09 Alcohol 52
1.10 The 365 Rule 57
1.11 Selective Rationalization 62
1.12 Perception is Reality 65
1.13 Worth Imitating 71
1.14 Courtesy And Respect 73
1.15 The Creative Process 76
1.16 Fear Vs. Panic 82
1.17 Personality Types 89
1.18 Bullies 99
1.19 Delegation 107
1.20 Management By Walking Around 121
1.21 Pick Your "Things" 125
1.22 Decision Making 128

1.23 Training 133
1.24 Communication 135
1.25 Coaching and Counseling 139
1.26 Documentation 146
1.27 Firing Someone 150
1.28 Public Speaking 154
1.29 Writing Skills 158
1.30 Meetings 160
1.31 Planners 164
1.32 Goals Lists 169
1.33 Now 172
1.34 Organization 177
1.35 Work Ethic 180
1.36 Financials/Controllers 186
1.37 False Comparisons 190
1.38 Negotiation 193
1.39 Push Back 201
1.40 Yes, We Can't 207
1.41 The Power of "No" 211
1.42 Parachutes 216
1.43 Tools 221
1.44 Lobster 224
1.45 Sops 226
1.46 Kiss 228
1.47 Office Politics and Back Stabbing 230
1.48 Effective Immediately 233
1.49 It's Already Been Done 236
1.50 When in Doubt—Hire A Professional 238
1.51 Hiring Staff 241
1.52 Money Doesn't Just Talk 243

1.53 It's All About The Money 247
1.54 Thank Yous 251
1.55 Perspective 256
1.56 Trouble 259
1.57 No Try 264
1.58 Prepare To Fail 267
1.59 Rating Your Department and/or Yourself 270
1.60 The Truth 276
1.61 Love 284
1.62 If It's Not Fun 292
1.OH Christmas Story 296

Dedication 305
About Me 307
Appendix/References 309

Acknowledgements

I would like to thank—with very few exceptions—my former bosses, managers and many of my former co-workers, for mostly showing me the "wrong way" to do almost everything.

I would like to thank myself, for doing almost everything the "wrong way" until I finally learned the "hard way" how to do things the "right way"—and for sticking with it until I did.

I would like to thank my dog. I don't have one at the moment, but if I did I would thank him. My periodic ownership of dogs over the years has taught me that it is possible to stay positive even when certain situations really seem to call for extreme pessimism. I think that is because dogs, in general, are the paradigm of unwavering positivism. How do they stay so positive?

Pessimistic humans like me could take a lesson.

Anyway, everyone loves his or her own dog, right? In fact, I've had a few dogs in the past that I loved a lot more than a lot of people—one Dalmatian in particular. He was one inspirational mutt, I can tell you that.

If I had a dog now, I am sure I'd probably feel the same. I need to get another one.

By the way, I don't love *your* dog—I don't care how "positive" it is. If I happen to be invited over to your house, please keep the damn thing away from me. My dog's kiss is magic. Your dog's kiss is a bacteria laden nightmare. My dog's bark is music. Your dog's bark is like someone running a 2-stroke blower right by my head.

Your kids fall into the same category. Please keep them away from me as well, especially if they're under the age of—oh say—sixteen. It's not that I don't like kids, it's just that I don't much like being around them until they've learned to be civilized. Screaming 2 year olds? Ugh! I don't care how "cute" they are.

If you have cats, I'm not even coming over—period!

Where were we? Oh, yes…

I would like to thank my wife, who thinks I am the smartest person she's ever met. She's wrong, of course. But ask me if I care.

Lastly, and far more seriously, I would like to thank those very few and very rare individuals that I have simply had the honor of knowing, who—almost always by example—taught me not only the "right way" to do things, but *how to be a better human being*. And, almost by default, a much better manager!

And yes, Mom, wherever you are now, you are definitely on that list.

Forward

I invent nothing. I rediscover.
      –Auguste Rodin

Okay. So why would I take on the daunting task of writing a book about management?

Why even bother? Aren't there already a go-zillion already out there?

What even gives me the right? The qualifications?

Why?

Well, because I think I'm pretty smart about management. In fact, I think I'm the best *overall* manager I've ever come across in the over four decades that I've been engaged in my profession. I'm not saying that there might not be a bunch of managers out there that are *way* better than me—it's just that I haven't run across any—and I've been around the block a few times.

There, I said it!

In fact, that felt pretty good.

Let me say it again:

I am a *great* manager.

Why do I think that?

Because almost everyone I've ever managed in the 40 plus years that I've been doing so *has told me so*—and I've managed a bunch. In fact, I've had a few of them tell me that their entire careers were radically and positively affected by working for me.

It's probably not true, but it sure is flattering.

Oh sure, there have also been some folks that have said some *not-so-nice* things about ole Dave Frazier, but I'm pretty confident that even though they might not like some things about me—like, perhaps, the fact that I *fired* them—most of them would still attest to my skills as an excellent manager.

And, I think that I've figured out the "why"—so I feel compelled to put it on "paper."

By the way, if my statement about being a "great manager" seems a bit braggadocious—too "in your face"—or a bit narcissistic, consider this:

Would you want to hear about how to become a great manager from someone who wasn't—or at least didn't *think* he was?

Exactly.

Anyway, if it makes you feel better, try this:

I am a *terrible* manager, but I know *how* to be a great one, so pull up a chair and listen the F up!

Better?

That's what I thought—but either statement works for me.

What specific profession are you so "great at" as a manager you might ask?

Hospitality.

Now, I hope you won't immediately scoff and hold that against me.

I know that the hospitality field is not generally viewed by most—*including me*—as the pinnacle of career choices, but I'll maintain that it's probably one of the hardest of all to manage. In fact, I can't think of any other business that employs a much more diverse group of people with as many diverse backgrounds, ethnicities and various levels of education.

Trying to get them all to cooperate as a team is no piece of cake, I can tell you that.

Anyway, this book is not really about hotels or the hotel business per se—so don't let it stop you from turning the next page.

What this book *is* about is how to effectively manage people. More to the point, a lot of what this book is about is how to *effectively manage your own self.*

Further, I think that the stuff I'm going to talk about in the next few pages would work just as well for you if you are in the grocery business, trying to launch a man to the moon, or running a brothel.

I also think that my formula applies to the boomers, the X'rs, the Y's and Z's, the oh-so-fragile millennials, and perhaps to the even more fragile generations that seem to be following! It might even be great in the military, but since I was never in the military, I'm reluctant to say.

However, the same principles seem to apply regardless *because they involve people.*

And, the principles are simple.

Most management books I've read—and I've read a lot—try to be too complex. Sometimes, it's as if the Ph. D's that have written them are just trying to show off. I get it. They've spent a long time educating themselves and they probably still have huge student loans to pay off. Good for them! If you want to plow through 450 pages of management "science" go for it.

This book is just meant to be a *management primer*—nothing more.

If it helps, think of it this way:

If I were attempting to write a book about dieting rather than one about management, it wouldn't have a clever title and it certainly wouldn't be a 250 or 300-page dissertation on the way "fat molecules interact with blood cells."

It would be much shorter and probably have a title more like this:

Stop Eating So Much!

Anyway, I *definitely* have no qualifications to write anything about dieting, and if you witnessed what I eat on a regular basis, you would more than agree.

However, regarding my educational bona fides:

Many moons ago, and by no small miracle, I somehow gained admittance to and *graduated* from Chico State California—which I am proud to say at the time was rated the #1 party school in America—with a Bachelor's degree in Philosophy and another in English Literature.

During my college years, I worked full time and drank full time and paid cash for everything including my tuition, so I didn't have any student debt when I finally finished—just a really bad hangover. Really bad. I'll let you be the judge if I got anything out of my rather dubious education and the two sheepskins I have hanging on my wall to prove it.

I've always said the *only* thing college really taught me was *how to teach myself something*—but that in and of itself is a pretty valuable tool don't you think?

It also taught me that you *can* maintain a very high GPA while being half in the bag—parents beware!

Anyway, we've all heard this phrase a million and one times:

Keep it simple stupid!

Yep.

There's a reason why that phrase has always had staying power.

So let's cut the "intellectual" crap. People are people. And, what makes them "go" or "not go" is pretty simple.

Here's the good news:

If you want to be a really great manager, then there are really only a few basic principles you need to follow.

Here's the rub:

Most of them are *very* hard to follow!

And, if you happen to be an inherent asshole, they're going to be nearly *impossible* to follow.

Fortunately for me, my asshole-ism apparently is not "inherent"—at least not the better part of it. But, I've had to make a lot of adjustments.

Lastly, let me make this admission:

Nothing I'm going to say in the following pages is new. Forget college; it's all stuff your mommy or daddy or your kindergarten teacher probably should have taught you.

Obviously, many of you—*including me*—weren't listening back then, so we try again.

Did I mention that management is a lot about repetition?

Might as well get started.

1.01 How?

Exactly.

How do I get "these people" to do what I want them to do *because they want to do it?*

As a manager, that's the real question, isn't it?

The key part of that "how" question, of course, being "*because they <u>want</u> to do it.*"

Later, we'll add a little onto that by saying—"*because they want to do it for <u>you</u>!*"

By the way, I say "these people" because it's not just the people working for us that we need cooperation from in life, right? It's virtually everybody.

More on that later.

Now, almost anyone can point a gun at someone and get "him" or "her" to do "something."

That's easy. The concept is, after all, the origin of the term "gunpoint management."

But that method of inspiring cooperation more or less disappeared over a century ago—at least in most of the more civilized portions of the planet—so managers have since been faced with the problem of getting people to do things because they *want to do it.*

That's not to say that gunpoint management has completely gone away. Some managers—mostly very bad ones—still try to use various forms of it. Maybe that's just the way they were taught by other very bad managers.

Maybe, they're "boomers"—i.e., dinosaurs—like me that still sometimes cling to the false notion that just because you're *paying* someone, they should do what you ask them to do, regardless of *how you ask them.*

"Back in the good old days…"

Yeah, right!

By the way, another interpretation of gunpoint management is simply "fear" or the attempt to create it.

Some of the old "fear" tactics include:

Bad mood boss syndrome.

Write-ups and/or the threat of them.

Critical and embarrassing memos.

Scoldings—both public and private.

"Effective immediately" announcements.

Forced adherence to S.O.P. manuals that mostly have nothing to do with anything.

Revocation of benefits or pay—or the threat of revocation.

Constant threat of firing—direct or indirect.

Belittlement, ridicule and other nasty things.

Etc.

Etc.

Etc.

I'm going to talk more about all of the above in a minute, but suffice it to say, that if your management "toolbox" consists primarily of the tactics listed above or anything like it you need to *throw that toolbox away*—or "shit-can" it if you prefer.

Those tactics might have worked okay back in the days when people were more fearful of losing their jobs. Now, they're more likely to sue you for harassment as they walk out the door with their middle finger extended high above their head.

If you feel that you *must* manage that way because that style is "in-your-bones" or it's "just the way you are," you might even want to reevaluate your career path entirely and save a bunch of people from a lot of needless suffering, because you should not be overseeing anyone. Your era ended a few decades ago!

Hey, I know… maybe you could become a reality TV star!

1.02 Humility

On the highest throne in the world, we still sit only on our own bottom.
–Michel de Montaigne

First off, let's just start by choking down a big spoonful of humility shall we?

Note: I'm doing this for a reason. In fact, every word I'm writing is for a specific reason, just in case you've already begun to wonder.

PS—if you skipped my "acknowledgements" or "forward" to this book, please stop everything and *go back and read them now*! They are critical to setting the proper "tone" for what I am going to try to achieve here.

Go ahead, I'll wait…

Back again?

Have you determined that much of what you're about to read might be laced with sarcasm?

Bingo.

You get an A for reading comprehension so far.

Oh, you're too fragile for a little indirect sarcasm? You don't appreciate my "tude"?

Stop reading.

See if I care.

I wrote this book for "fun," not to get you to like me.

But, before you turn off your Kindle or slam the hard copy shut, let me say this:

If you can't handle *me*, then you should probably go back to your line job or stay in your room. The world is full of people like me, and some of them are likely to end up being your boss at one point or another. Hell, some of them might end up being your spouse if you're not careful.

I'm just trying to prepare you for the inevitable.

Now where were we?

Oh yeah:

e a manager—any manager, at any salary range, g a manager who makes a *go-friggin-zillion-dollars* you are still simply an *em-ploy-ee* of someone who

Now, that "not-an-employee" person might not be your immediate report. In fact, the company you work for might be so big you might not even know who exactly the heck "he" or "she" or "they" are that are *not* employees, but somewhere up the corporate or privately held LLC river your own little management boat is floating on, is/are the guy/s *actually controlling the dam*—and their title is not "employee," or "general manager," or even perhaps "chairman of the board."

This is their title:

Owner or major stockholder.

How about in government you might ask?

I would say that if you're not the governor of a state or the president of the United States… forget about it. You are still essentially a "proletariat," perhaps with a big title like CEO or Senior Vice President or Senator, but *still* a proletariat. Even those guys/gals high up in politics are supposedly working for someone, although they seldom act like it, especially when they've just been elected.

Here's my point:

If you are not the *owner* or *major stockholder* or the POTUS, you are working for someone or some entity who is so much smarter than you, it's *amazing*.

Why, you might ask yourself? Why are they so much smarter than me?

Because, they are the ones *who cannot be fired*!

They are the ones who bought the business, built the business, put up the money for the business, or had the idea for it in the first place. Or, they are the ones who got elected to the highest office possible and are probably at least good for a four-year run of "cannot be fired." Or, etc.

Most importantly—they are the ones who *pulled the trigger* when it was time to pull it. They are the ones with the *really* big boat!

Now, maybe some of them only have a small business and their boat doesn't look all that big.

Maybe they really aren't that smart.

Maybe they were just extremely lucky.

Smart or not, lucky or not, here is the major thing they don't have that you do—*a boss*!

Now, I've worked with a lot of guys who thought they were pretty smart—even mid-level guys—who thought they were "pretty big stuff" when they were actually still paddling around in really small corporate canoes *that they didn't even own.*

In fact, if we have had to climb any management ladder in our lives, we have all been victims of "those" kind of guys, haven't we? The guys who "know-it-all" and think they are really smarter than anyone else in the room; paddling their little "borrowed" canoes around and screaming either directly or indirectly at the world about how great they are.

Senior VP of what?

Spoiler alert for non-owners and/or non-major stockholders or non-Presidents of the United States:

> You are not exactly a rocket scientist!

I'm not saying this to be mean and nasty. I'm saying it for a very good reason:

> You cannot be a really great manager without a good dose of self-evaluation and humility.

Shoot, I could make you a list of a hundred smarty pants that I've had to deal with over the years—but I'm old—and you might just be getting started.

Anyway, here's the point—again:

If you don't *own* the place, or at least have a controlling interest, *you* are not that smart.

Also good to know:

If the person you work for isn't the owner or doesn't have a controlling interest in the company, *they* are not that smart— *but be careful, they still might be a whole lot smarter than you!*

Also:

If someone you work with is a blood relative of the owner—*be very careful*. You can be sure that even if they aren't smarter than you, they are *way* more important than you.

At this point in my life, I've taken the "owner" concept one step further just to make myself feel better about my own failures:

Even if the guy who's acting real smart around me *is* an owner—if he isn't flying around privately in his own Gulf Stream—well… he still ain't no Jeff Bezos or Bill Gates, so even he/she isn't all that smart.

I know it's a pretty empty argument, but it makes me feel better.

To summarize:

If you are not the "owner"—then this would suggest that *you are not that smart.*

Even if you *are* the owner—then unless you are tooling around in a nice Lear or Gulfstream and are not worried at all about how much it's costing you or your company—then even *you* are not that smart.

Why do I say this?

Because, as long as you realize you're "*not-that-smart*" then you might remain *humble,* and that is important because it will help you to remain *teachable.*

And, just to be clear, for all of my earlier bragging about what a great manager I think I am—know this:

I don't think I'm very smart.

If I were smart I'd be rich.

If I were *really* smart I'd be "private jet rich" or be writing this on the desk in the Oval office!

Now, I have to admit, for quite a few years, I *wanted* to be the smartest guy in the room—I really did.

And I tried hard.

I can recall sitting in meeting after meeting with my professional counterparts—most of them male of course—all pawing the conference table like a bunch of hungry lions trying to demonstrate their individual brilliance.

For a while, I thought I had a chance to make it into the "smart guy" club.

Fun fact:

When I was young, I was actually placed in a class for the "gifted."

At around 11 or 12 years of age, my mother and my teachers had begun to wonder why I was reading at practically college level, so they gave me a battery of tests trying to determine my IQ.

Apparently I did well on the tests, because I was immediately thrust into a "special class" with a few other kids who had also done well.

Now, I was already becoming pretty anti-social by that point and I didn't like any of the kids in the class—nerds! So, much to my mother's chagrin, I basically sabotaged anything those well intentioned adults were trying to do for me and dropped out.

Anyway, you might think given that background that I might have had a shot.

Nope. Apparently not.

In subsequent years, I've banged my head on so many things both figuratively and literally, that whatever brainpower I might have had at one time—well, it has pretty much been vaporized.

Occasionally, whenever I *really* need it, I seem to be able to conjure some of my youthful "brilliance" back up, but mostly—it's gone! Gone!

So much so, in fact, that in almost any setting I have now determined that I must be the *dumbest guy in the room*, especially based on what everyone else's priorities seem to be.

It's okay. I've gotten comfortable with it

Do you know what I'm shooting for now?

I'm working on not being the biggest *asshole* in the room!

Much easier—but I think I can just forget about that private jet.

1.03 It's Not About The Money

Speaking of getting "rich":

You're not in this management "thing" for the money, right?

Right?

Because I can think of a bunch of different ways for making money that would be a way better use of your time:

Buy or start a business and succeed.

Go to an ivy-league school and become a hedge fund manager for a major company.

Become a great salesperson that works for big commissions.

Buy lots of lottery tickets and get lucky.

If your parents happen to be rich, be nice to them.

Etc.

Here's the thing:

Once you are in the management game, you are basically screwed money wise. You are going to get an annual raise of somewhere between 3-5% and your bonus will be the same year-in and year-out plus a couple of points if you're lucky.

At some point, if you're unlucky, there will be an economic downturn or some other business event where your bosses will be "forced" to "temporarily" freeze your salary and to cancel or radically reduce your bonus.

"You should feel fortunate that you still have your job," they will say. And, if they are even halfway proficient negotiators they'll get *you* to say it and believe it!

The only way you'll get a bigger financial lift than that is if you get promoted or switch companies. And, if you do get promoted or go to a new company, you will immediately be back to the 3-5% annual scenario.

Incidentally, not to make you feel worse, but if you factor CPI/inflation into your measly 3-5% raise—which typically hovers annually between 2-3%—well, you do the math. Even with a 5% annual, it will take you somewhere around 35 years to double your salary!

What about all those highly compensated CEO's you ask?

"I'm going to become one of them," you say?

Yes, and I'm going to be drafted by the NFL.

Look, I'm not trying to bum you out. I'm just trying to be real.

Early on in our careers, we get used to our "regular" paychecks. Then, we have a family and *need* our paychecks. Then, we take out a mortgage, buy a couple of cars, and run up our credit cards until we are basically screwed.

Sometimes we are really stupid and buy a boat!

And, with every passing year, our tolerance for risk diminishes.

In any salary "negotiation," we are not really negotiating anything. *Our boss is just telling us what our raise is going to be.*

That's because we seldom have "walk away power" when we have that annual discussion.

Or…

Maybe we just like where we work and don't want to leave, or we just had a kid and we can't afford to leave, or we're waiting to become fully vested, or…

Or… drum roll…

Maybe you were smart enough to go to work for a company that provides stock options, profit sharing, or some other *real* form of potential long-term compensation. Good for you!

Now, I'm not saying that you can't make a very good living as a manager.

I have.

I'm just saying that if what you're doing is really "about the money" then you should do something that is really "about the money."

Here's my point and I'll let this go:

As a manager, you are not in this for the money!

You are in this for *the pure joy of being the best at what you do*!

And, so you can make that friggin' boat payment!

1.04 It's Your Fault

Now that we've discussed some of your shortcomings and mine, let's figure out whose fault it is that *we are who we are.*

Drum roll:

It's *yours*!

And no one else's.

Let me repeat:

Whatever "it" is—it's *your* fault.

Whether you are a first time manager, or you've been at this for a while, this is another important "truth" to have in your arsenal.

In fact—forget management—it's a crucial tool to have in your life!

Period.

Example:

When I'm whining and moaning, like *I often do* because someone messed something up or something bad happened, it's always good for me to remember *who* exactly got me into whatever uncomfortable situation I'm in.

Here's a short list of them:

My financial situation.

My family.

The way my department or business runs—or doesn't.

My relationship with my boss and/or my staff.

The company I work for.

My dog. (As I mentioned, I don't have a dog right now, but I'm going to get one, and I already know it will be nothing *but* a problem.)

Etc.

Yes, I often ask myself, *who* exactly did get me into this situation?

Answer to myself:

You did, silly!

Here's the point:

As a manager, whatever is going on in your department or your business—aside from the weather or nuclear annihilation—*it's your fault.*

Personal life—same thing.

You took the job.

You've kept the job.

You hired the person.

You did/didn't give the right instructions.

You did/didn't plan correctly.

You got the damn dog.

You married them.

You bought the boat!

Family? Okay, maybe you didn't choose your family, but now that you're an adult…

Why do I say this?

Because in order to fix a problem it helps to know whose fault it is.

Now, once again:

Whose fault is it?

Answer:

Yours! It's yours—*even* if it isn't!

Everywhere I go, there I am.

If you're looking for the "elephant in the room," go find a mirror!

You don't like your staff?

Fire them.

You don't like your weight?

Go on a diet.

You don't like your job?

Quit.

You don't like your dog?

Train him or kill him.

Family?

You already know what I'm going to say about that.

And, for God's sake, sell the boat!

Incidentally, we might be able to make a case that all of the above is really our parent's fault or that we were raised in poverty or whatever—but would that really get us anywhere?

Nope.

It's okay.

As we've discussed, not everyone can be a super-rich, super-smart go-zillionaire!

As a manager, you can take some consolation in the fact that *you are needed!*

We are like cops and first responders and school principals. We make sure that when someone calls 911, there is someone on duty who will answer the phone. We make sure that when someone sends their kids to class, there is someone there to teach them. We make sure that when someone goes to the store, there is food on the shelves, or that the trains run on time, or the "fast food" is fast.

In fact, if you think about it, managers *really* are what make the world go round.

And…

Great managers make it go better.

1.05 The Customer

Okay.

Now that I have you feeling real good about yourself, let me ask you this question:

Who is *your* most important customer?

No, it is *not* the "*person in front of you.*"

Boring.

Try again.

Wait…

Let me rephrase the question:

Who are your *most important* customers—plural—and in *what order* from most important to least important?

Wait…

Before you answer, let's define "customer."

I define them like this:

People that we are of service to.

Now, let's try this again.

Who, then, are the most important people we are *of service to*—in order of importance?

Who is number 1?

I'm going to submit a crazy idea:

It's *you*!

Yes—*you*! Numero Uno! *YOU*!

Isn't that great!

Let me explain:

If you don't treat yourself as your own *most important customer*, you cannot be in an effective position to treat any of your other "most" important customers down the line.

Right?

Examples:

If you don't prioritize taking care of your health.

If you don't prioritize taking care of your personal responsibilities.

If you don't prioritize taking care of your own finances.

And—this is *paramount*:

If you don't prioritize engaging in the things that *make you happy*.

Now, do I really need to spend a lot of time trying to explain why taking care of your self is a *critical* component of being able to take care of others, or can we move on?

By the way, if you try to tell me your kids or your husband or your friggin' cat are *more important than you*—I'm going to scream!

Okay.

After *you*, who's next most important on the "customer" roster?

No, it's not your boss, although we'll get to that.

Drum roll:

It's your spouse or your SO or partner whatever you like to call them.

Don't have one?

Then save the #2 spot for when you do.

Once again, do I need to spend a lot of time defending this? How the heck can you be great at work if your SO situation isn't right? I mean… we are still talking about "great" vs. "good," right?

And, assuming you have a SO, how could anything besides your own wellbeing take priority over making sure that your SO is treated as the most important customer in your life.

Now, if you want to jump on me about referring to yourself or your spouse as a "customer" go ahead—but you would be needlessly missing the point over a matter of semantics.

Get over it.

Next:

Your kids if you have them.

Obviously—although I've known more than a few parents who don't act that way.

Next:

The rest of your dysfunctional family.

By the way, I only say "dysfunctional" because I have *never* known a family that wasn't dysfunctional to one degree or another.

Feel better about yours now?

Oh, your family isn't dysfunctional?

Will you invite me over?

I want to meet them!

Next:

Your friends.

Here's the exception:

I might be willing to let you prioritize your friends over some of the rest of your dysfunctional family because *you might be completely justified in doing so.*

Up to you.

Next:

Your dog if you have one.

Regarding cats: I only like cats that are *never* allowed in the house and are forced to catch rodents and other undesirable creatures to earn their own living. Cats don't even come close to being any kind of most important customer. Some mangy fish in some dirty aquarium would take priority over a cat!

Note: I happen to have a large aquarium and my fish—especially those that are sleeping upside down at the top of the tank—are some of the nicest and best-behaved pets you are ever unlikely to meet.

Here's the point:

You cannot be of "great" service to anyone if your *own personal life* is not at least somewhat squared away.

Besides, what would the point of that be anyway?

Isn't the achievement of personal happiness the most important goal in life?

If you want to argue *that* point, please do it with someone else.

Confession time:

I'm not really what you would call a "happy person" by nature. I've met some of them—and I am definitely *not* one of them.

Inherent malcontent?

Terminal pessimist?

Perhaps.

Anyway:

In order to get "happy" I've had to *learn* how to spend more of my time looking at the "half-full" part of the glass rather than the "half-empty."

It's not easy. For some people maybe it is.

For me?

Not so much.

I'm just saying this: *practice makes perfect.* I get better and better at it all the time.

Sometimes, just for the heck of it, I'll take a glass out of the cupboard, fill it halfway with water or whatever, and then just sit and stare at it for a while.

One thing I figured out by doing this little exercise is that the glass isn't going to get any "fuller" by me simply staring at it.

I have to *do* something!

For me, thinking good thoughts is a choice.

Focusing on the "half-full" or the "half-empty" part is a choice.

Why is this important?

Well, for one thing, why would I want to unnecessarily spend my life miserable for no good reason?

Now, we all probably know some folks who seem to thrive on misery, but...

Really?

Here is one of my big life lessons:

Life is hard.

It's designed that way.

Lots and lots of problems.

And, just when you solve one, up pops another.

Living is difficult.

And, if you don't like it, time is going to take care of that particular "problem" for you soon enough.

In the meantime, we could all learn a lesson from dogs.

Okay, now that I've lectured you on the obvious importance of striving to live a happy life over a miserable one, let's talk about why it's particularly important if you want to be a great manager:

Because people can smell discontent and misery like a bad odor.

You can, right?

News flash:

Everyone else can too!

Let me ask you this:

Do you think anyone *wants* to work for a terminally malcontent person? And yes, I am fully aware of the fact that many people do. But, do they really *want* to and would they if they thought they had a choice?

If you happen to be stuck working for one, do you consider him or her to be a great manager?

Answer:

Probably not so much.

Let's recap:

Unless you put yourself first, you cannot be a great manager.

Unless you put the rest of your personal life first, you cannot be a great manager.

Unless you can more or less find your own "happy place" most of the time in life you cannot be a great manager.

What's that smell?

Is it the sour stench of terminal discontent?

Or...

The sweet perfume of happiness?

Note: I am not saying that some people don't have terrible lives. I've known some, like we all have, that have had *terrible* things happen to them; loss of a child, terminal disease, abusive relationships, etc. Heck, I've actually had the privilege of knowing a concentration camp survivor.

Bad, right? Right! *But that's not me.*

My life—no matter how tough I might think it's been—has been a comparative piece of cake.

So I often ask myself this rhetorical question:

How can a concentration camp survivor find happiness and I can't?

Where were we?

Oh yeah.

Most important customer.

Now, I think, we're finally ready to talk about "work."

So:

At work, who is your most important customer?

No, again, it's not "*the friggin' person in front of you!*"

Ugh!

Well, I guess it could be, but *only under one circumstance.*

That "person" in front of you happens to be *your boss*!

Okay, admittedly, this took me a while to finally figure out. I think it might have been due to the fact that most of my bosses early in my career didn't seem to know WTF they were doing.

When you think about it, it *is* rather obvious though, right?

Your boss is the one you are actually being *paid to serve.*

More importantly, your boss is the one who holds the "keys" to your professional kingdom.

Why then, would you not want them to think that *you* are the best thing since proverbial sliced bread?

Now, I know that a lot of you probably hold or have held your otherwise incompetent boss in contempt at one time or another. We all could do their job better than they ever could, right?

I'll probably mention this again, but here is a very important observation regarding your boss:

I believe you can actually learn as much or more from a bad boss than a good one, and since most of mine have been questionable, this has been fortunate for me.

We'll discuss more about that later.

Anyway:

If you happen to be blessed with a "bad" boss—*don't do what they do* now or in the future when you've finally stolen their job!

In the meantime:

Whoever and whatever their strengths or failings might be—*make them "love" you!*

You already consider yourself to be a pretty good manager, right? I mean, secretly, half the time you think you're actually better than your bosses, right?

Then put those skills to work with them:

How do I get my boss to do what I want him/her to do?

Once again, the fact that the most important customer at work has to be your boss seems obvious.

Is it obvious to you? If it wasn't before it should be now.

Okay, let's move on.

Next most important customer, please?

Yes!

Your staff!

Why is your staff so important?

Obviously, as a manager, they are the determining factor in demonstrating whether or not you know what the heck you are doing!

Later on, we're actually going to discuss how to manage them, but we are not ready yet.

Finally, least important customer?

The lady on aisle A.

Yes. Bingo!

Now, I'm not saying "lady on isle A" is not important. She is, after all, the one who is ultimately going to pay the bills for your company. I'm just saying she's not *your* most important customer.

She is your *staff's* most important customer! That is, she is your staff's most important customer *right after you!*

By the way, if the lady on isle A *is* your most important customer—you've mismanaged something.

Let's recap.

Most important customer in your personal life?

You.

Most important customer in your professional life?

Your boss.

Close second?

Your staff.

The end.

Period.

Oh, yeah.

Your glass is chronically "half-empty"?

Get a bigger glass.

Smaller glass?

Anyway, you get the point.

1.06 Bad Managers

Since I brought this subject up, I want to just briefly touch on it *again* so everyone who works for one can quit complaining:

Most people end up working for really "bad" managers at least once if not several times in their careers.

Suck it up. That's the way it is.

In their defense, most managers who are bad at what they do *don't even know it.*

Heck, I am sometimes bad at what I do *and I know it—and I do it anyway!*

Also, like most people, you probably think you could do a way better job than *anyone doing almost anything*, let alone your boss or your manager—so you're already predisposed to thinking they're "bad."

If you have a good dose of Amiable in you, you are *positive* you could do a way better job and you'll tell anyone besides your boss about it.

Just admit it and we can move on.

We'll get to Amiables in a minute.

Anyway, for those of you who work for a "bad" manager, I bring you great tidings of joy!

You have two options:

Quit.

Or…

Pay attention to *exactly* what that manager is doing that you think is so "bad" and make a note of it so *you don't do it when it's your turn*—if ever—to take the helm!

I tell my staff—when they are moaning about something or I just have a sense that they think they could do my job way better than me—to pay close attention to all of my "bad" management tactics and when *they* eventually move on into a management position, they can feel free to manage *their* department or business or whatever just the way *they* want—and the sooner the better!

"Take my job! Please!"

That usually shuts them up!

Here's my point:

Most managers "learned" to be managers totally by experiment and/or accident. Someone thought they knew something or maybe—like me—they just consistently showed up for work so they were promoted from "the line."

Over time, some of them learn to be good managers and some of them don't seem to learn anything.

Sink or swim.

1.07 Glass Houses

Sorry.

I promise that sooner or later I'll get to actually managing your staff.

But first, let's talk some more about personal conduct.

In fact, let's talk a lot about it.

So...

Maybe you just got promoted.

Maybe, you've been a "line" employee for a while and this is your first management gig.

Maybe you've been a manager for years and this following fact has never dawned on you.

I have important and critical news:

Nothing you do from now on as far as work is concerned is private.

If you don't believe me, ask yourself this question:

Was anything any former boss did or said missed by you or anyone else working for them at the time?

No.

Here's my point:

Now that you are a manager you are also:

THE BOSS

As a result, you are now swimming around in a very clear fishbowl—*by yourself.*

Your underlings are now going to know and start paying a lot of attention to the following:

When you go to the bathroom.

If it was #1 or #2, what it smelled like, and *did you wash your hands afterward?*

When you get to work and when you leave.

Nose hair.

If you missed a spot shaving—on your face or your legs depending.

If your car is clean or dirty.

If the interior of your car is clean or dirty.

Who you're dating or married to—or both.

What you said and *the way you said it* to anybody!

Etc.

Realize this:

From now on—like it or not—just by *being* a manager, you've just turned up the scrutiny of everyone as it pertains to *you*. In fact, you might as well have put yourself under a high-powered microscope.

From now on don't think that anything you do will go unnoticed or un-noted *and behave accordingly.*

I could give you tons of examples of bosses doing things they thought no one was going to notice—things which I am sure *they would not have done* had they been aware that others were watching, particularly their subordinates.

Let's just do one:

Many years ago, I was out having lunch with some of my corporate level counterparts at a local restaurant. On our way back to the office, we spotted a far more senior manager in our company pulling in to a liquor store and parking his car.

Now, I'm not saying it was right, but our curiosity got the better of us so we pulled over and watched. He was, after all, much higher up the management chain and we were curious.

Anyway, everything about his behavior as he got out of his car seemed suspicious. He was sort of nervously looking around, etc. We watched him go in to the store and shortly emerge with a bag that obviously contained a bottle of something. Then, he got in his car and took a big pull from whatever bottle was in the bag.

In his defense, it might have been a bottle of sparkling water. Maybe he was just thirsty? Unfortunately, this person already had a reputation of being "half-in-the-bag" most of the time anyway, so you can imagine our own conclusion.

Here's the point:

If you are not comfortable with your actions literally ending up on the 6 o'clock news—*don't do them.* I don't care how clever you think you are, someone, somehow is going to figure out what you are up to.

Why? Because as *the boss,* anything you do is BIG NEWS to your staff.

Did I say don't do it?

What I meant is don't do anything you don't want your staff to know about.

If you are having an affair, your staff will know.

If you pick your nose, your staff will know.

If you lie, cheat and steal, your staff will know.

Conversely:

If you *never* do any of the above, your staff *will know that too.*

1.08 Sex

Yes!

Sex, sex, and more sex!

But not at work—not if you are a manager.

Especially not *if you're a manager*!

Guilty.

Okay, I admit it. When I was young and single and just a "mid-manager" in the hospitality industry, I dated some of my co-workers, even some in *my own* department.

Yikes!

In my defense: it was the early '80s and there was a different attitude back then about sex in the workplace. It was more "laissez faire" so to speak on both sides of the gender aisle—much more! Also, since I was literally working 60-70 hours a week, there wasn't much opportunity to meet or date anyone I wasn't working with.

Anyway, I was lucky that none of my escapades ever turned into a scandal.

One reason:

I never asked anyone "out" more than once—and I was pretty good at making sure there was some obvious interest before I asked anyone anything. Sometimes, they even asked me!

Basically, regarding dating, I followed this important rule:

"No" meant no. Period.

And, I followed that rule *religiously*!

Now, did "everyone" know that I was dating some of my co-workers?

Yes. Absolutely. *I was a manager*!

But, did they know *for sure?*

No. I was never "obvious" about it in the workplace and had all of my escapades *off* property. And, once again, it was the '80s and I wasn't the general manager!

In short, I didn't consider myself to be *the boss*. I considered the general manager of the hotel to be *the boss*. At least, that's how I rationalized it at the time.

Did I say "rationalizations" are dangerous?

More on that topic later…

What about now?

No.

Don't do it.

Did I say don't do it?

DON'T DO IT!

I am going to say this:

Never as a general manager or corporate officer have I dated anyone on my staff, had an affair with anyone on my staff, or made obnoxious comments of a sexual nature directed at anyone on my staff.

Have I made obnoxious comments?

Yes!

Were they wrong?

Yes.

But, *never* to one of my staff directly. "Locker room talk" that fortunately for me, has apparently never left the "locker room." I've been lucky.

Have I ever had one of my staff members come on to me?

Yes!

Was it hard to turn them down?

Yes! Especially when those invitations occurred during the brief moments I was single or might as well have been.

Am I glad I resisted?

Yes.

Why?

Because now, after all of these years—and I'm talking over 30—I have a "perfect" track record of not sexually harassing my staff, not trying to have sex with my staff, and not actually having sex with my staff.

That's a pretty long time.

Does my staff know?

Yes.

They know *everything*!

This fact, incidentally, might just come in handy someday if I am ever falsely accused of any of the above—don't ya think?

Here's the point:

How many people—*and men, unfortunately, I'm speaking mostly to you*—have ruined themselves over some scandal regarding sex?

How many otherwise good or even excellent managers have ended up looking stupid and/or have been fired for some sexual escapade gone bad?

I've lost count of the ones I've had to deal with during my career.

This naturally brings me to my next topic:

1.09 Alcohol

Okay, I'm just going to say this regarding alcohol and your employment:

No!

Not if you want to be "great."

It's interesting to me that although attitudes regarding sex and sexual harassment have changed over the years, it seems like not much has changed regarding attitudes about alcohol consumption. If there ever was a sacred cow, its name would be alcohol.

For example:

The company dinner or the company party? Lunch with clients?

Let 'er rip!

It's still somehow acceptable to drink all you want—*until it's not.*

Do you want to stay out of trouble?

No alcohol.

And by that, I mean no alcohol *as it pertains to your work environment.*

It makes even the most conservative and careful person stupid. It makes people say things and do things they're going to regret.

"But I *have* to drink," you say. "It's part of my job."

No, you don't.

Full disclaimer:

I was a food and beverage director of a major hotel and didn't drink. In fact, I haven't had a cocktail since I was 23 years old. I have no "off" button, as they say.

Anyway, if anyone could claim that drinking was part of the job, there would be no one better to claim it than a food and beverage director at a major hotel, right? You have to pick the hard liquor you're selling, the wine you're selling and the beer you're selling. Purveyors are constantly stopping by with cases of the stuff begging you to sample them.

How then, did I manage to do my job as a food and beverage director without drinking?

Easy.

There are these things called "reviews." Or, I grabbed the dining room manager or the bar manager and had them taste the stuff, or…

Anyway, I promise not to harp on this much longer, but…

How many stories do you know about co-workers that have ended up with a proverbial "lamp-shade" on their heads around alcohol after the company dinner or the picnic? How many scandalous affairs?

I bet you know at least a few.

I could tell you a "million." Some of them are so classic and "funny" that they are never to be forgotten. They are especially funny *if you are not involved*!

In fact, I have friends in the business who, along with myself, take great joy in recounting outrageous incidents that occurred even *decades ago*.

"Remember when so-and-so did such-and-such?"

Ah ha haa!

Want to stay out of trouble?

Here's what I recommend:

If you feel you must!

One cocktail and *only* if it is at an evening event!

Did I say one?

I meant: *one*!

Did I say "evening" event?

I said: *evening event*!

No, not "late" lunch!

Example:

Let's say you're at some fancy-schmancy "work" dinner that is a "wine pairing"—which is synonymous with "let's get shit-faced"—six courses with a glass of something "wonderful" for each course.

One sip, each course. That's it! Taste it and set it aside.

And, if you can't pull that off then stay home, or just do what I do, and don't drink at all!

Drink water. Or soda. Or coffee.

Anyway, I have seen more careers ruined or at least negatively and permanently tempered from situations arising around the consumption of alcohol than I care to name—and so have you.

If you want to drink outside of the workplace, go for it.

If you drink in the workplace and you *never*—and I mean *never*—get into any kind of trouble around it, go for it.

There.

I'm done.

You're going to drink anyway.

But, when you end up swimming naked in the hotel pool or missing from the morning seminar because you got arrested the night before or you wake up in bed with someone who you definitely shouldn't be in bed with, don't say I didn't warn you.

Oh yeah, and *everyone* will know.

Did I say everyone?

Yes, *everyone*!

1.10 The 365 Rule

Speaking of "never," let's beat the proverbial dead horse of "never" a little more, shall we?

Did I also mention that management is a lot about repetition?

Anyway, you're not a line guy anymore, right?

You are a *manager*!

The 365 RULE is simply this:

Now that *you are a manager*, you absolutely can *never* lose your cool.

No tantrums.

No screaming.

No outrageous exhibitions of anger.

Never!

Not if you want to be "great."

The way I explain it is sort of crass, but it goes like this:

Let's say I'm perfect 364 days a year, but on the last day I go out in the parking lot in plain view of everyone, pull down my pants and take a crap in front of my staff and the world in general.

What will I be remembered for?

I don't think it's going to be for the 364 days I was "perfect."

I don't think that it would be the 364 days that I used the restroom like a normal civilized human.

I think it would be for that one day when I went *nut-zo* in the parking lot.

Try this example:

I'm a model citizen all year, but on the last day I murder someone.

You think my fellow citizens are going to just let that murder slide because I'm "good" most of the rest of the time?

Here's the point—again:

Being weird, mean, overly emotional and/or even inconsistent in our behavior is the dubious luxury of people *other than managers*.

No excuses.

No, "well I was having a bad day."

No, "sorry I just broke up with my girlfriend."

You can make up cheesy excuses or say those things all you want—but you can't be "great" if you do.

In fact, I don't think you can even be "good."

More likely—you're probably "bad."

I also sometimes characterize "getting weird or overly and negatively emotional" to my managers and staff this way:

"I am the highest paid person in the department/building/whatever and—fun fact—*my bosses are not paying me enough to get upset about anything.*

"Therefore, it is certain that they are not—and I'm not—paying *you* enough to get upset about anything."

Cool.

Calm.

Collected.

100% of the time.

That is the goal. But it is more than that—*it is the imperative.*

I once worked for a general manager who was nothing *but* emotional. He would get "mad" and he would get "glad."

For the staff, going to work was like getting on a—wait for it—*friggin' roller coaster and riding it in a dark tunnel*! We never quite knew what the day would bring as far as our boss's mood or what turn it might take.

Every once in a while he would even criticize me for not being "emotional enough" about my job, so one day he pissed me off to the point that I "showed" him what emotional looked like. He never mentioned my "lack of emotion" again.

Anyway, regardless of where *he* was emotionally, I know this:

He put everyone constantly on guard and—unfortunately—on edge.

Here's the kicker:

He was putting everyone on edge *for no good reason*!

Stop it!

Not *most* of the time. Not the *better part* of the time.

All of the time!

If it helps, think of yourself as a paramedic and that every day is an accident scene that you've just shown up at.

Would you want your paramedic freaking out and getting emotional as he or she attended to you?

Breaking down and crying?

Screaming and ranting, "Oh, my god, what should I do?"

I don't think so.

You want your doctor or paramedic to be a "rock."

You want to be a great manager?

Be the rock!

All of the time.

Every time.

365 days a year.

1.11 Selective Rationalization

I've indirectly touched on this already, but it's one of my favorite topics so I want to highlight it.

Here is my intro:

One of my favorite movies is called the Big Chill. In it, Jeff Goldblum plays this sort of sleazy character by the name of Michael Gold.

In one scene, "Michael" makes the argument that "selective rationalization" is more important than sex. When he gets pushback from the other characters, who all proclaim that "nothing is more important than sex," he says something like this:

"Oh yeah, ever try to go more than a week without a juicy selective rationalization?"

Here's my point:

Selective rationalizations are just that. They are mostly based on *only* the information—*true* or *false* or completely *ludicrous*—that supports them, while ignoring *facts* that *do not.*

Get it? Selective!

Really, most of the time, it's just weak justification for doing something we really know is stupid.

We all do it.

Some of us more than others.

For example:

I like to smoke. My selective rationalization for that is that I "hate" people, and that if I don't smoke I will "hate" them even more.

Now, obviously, I don't really hate people and smoking or not smoking has nothing at all to do with how I feel about anyone, but it "sounds" almost like a good justification.

Stupid, I know, but it works for me while it ignores all the more intelligent facts about why I shouldn't smoke.

Let's look at some more typical examples:

I was upset, that's why I "went off" on so and so.

I want to clean my car, but I just don't have the time.

I had a moment of weakness.

I meant to do…

Here's my point:

We all make lots of decisions in our lives based on selective rationalizations.

Just be aware of the fact that that is *what* you are doing *when* you are doing it.

The reason I point this out is because most people I know selectively rationalize without *being aware in the slightest that they are doing just that.*

And…

Here's the BIG reason:

Because SR's are the "keys to the kingdom" of bad behavior!

Beware!

1.12 Perception is Reality

I'm giving this subject a quick chapter just in case we miss it somewhere else.

Here is the gist of it:

No matter what you might "think" of yourself—how "great" you are, how "cool" you are, whatever—other people's perception of you has a great bearing on how you will be evaluated and responded to.

In the case of a manager, it's how he/she will/will not be followed.

For example:

What if you only missed work one time a year, but that somehow was always the day your regional boss decided to show up?

What if your office was always neat as a pin, except the day your boss decided to pay you a visit?

What if your department generally runs smoothly, except on the day your boss shows up?

You might think that you "never" miss work, or that you are "neat," or that your department really does run well.

News flash:

That's probably *not* what your boss thinks!

I'll give you another more personal one:

Over the years, for whatever reason, I've developed a "look." Okay, I guess we could call it a not-so-friendly countenance—perhaps a "scowl."

Anyway, whatever it is, people who don't know me and meet me for the first time almost always think I'm pissed off.

Worse, they often think I'm pissed off *at them*!

Now, I don't usually feel pissed off, but that doesn't matter. People in general *think* I am! I know this because they've told me so.

"You know, Mr. Frazier, when I first met you I thought you were pissed off."

So, over the years, since I can't seem to change the "look," I've had to compensate by being—ugh—overly "nice," especially when I first meet people. Unless, of course, I don't care or think it might be *to my advantage* for them to assume I'm a pissed off asshole.

Anyway, here's the point:

You can "think" you're neat, clean, well mannered, punctual, nice, or whatever. In fact, you can actually *be* all of those things most of the time.

But, it doesn't matter *if those around you don't think so.*

Disclaimer: If you are retired or otherwise don't have a reason to give a shit what other people think of you—fine.

Where were we?

Oh yeah, "perception":

It's just one more example why you need to concentrate on being "perfect" all of the time.

Caught with a messy desk?

Messy.

Caught unprepared?

Unprepared.

Caught screaming at some one?

Screamer.

Caught lying.

Liar.

Late for a couple of meetings?

Always late.

Etc.

Remember, we're talking about the difference between being "good" and "great."

By the way, can I just say something real quick about people who are chronically late for everything?

I just don't get it.

You know what's even weirder?

Have you noticed that the late folks are almost always exactly late the same amount of time?

There's the "always 10 minute late" people.

The always "15."

The always…

Anyway, you get the picture. There are certain individuals that you can almost set your watch by as far as "how late" they are going to be.

I mean, I'm not saying I've never been late for anything, but I have about a 99% record of being on time. I chalk it up to planning and *choosing* to be early rather than chance or risk being late.

Anyway, if you *are* one of "those" types I would advise you to stop it—now!

Figure out what your "chronically late" problem is and fix it.

Nothing is more annoying to those that are on time than someone who is not.

As long as you're constantly late, you can never be great.

In fact, you are more likely to be "perceived" as some kind of asshole.

Is there a difference between the way you perceive yourself and the way others perceive you?

Think about it.

1.13 Worth Imitating

If you want to be great—then emulate greatness.

Wow! What a simple concept, right?

When I was still a very young manager, I was transferred to a hotel run by a general manager by the name of Mike McCloud. Mike was probably only in his early forties at the time, but I was just in my early twenties, so I thought he was an "old guy."

Mike was one of these tall, strapping, good-looking men that had a Sean Connery 007 kind of aura about him; confident and prematurely graying at the temples, he definitely seemed to command the respect of everyone that worked for him.

Personally, the man was *so* imposing I was scared shitless of him.

Anyway, I don't remember the exact circumstances or even why this came up, but one day, early on in my time at that hotel, he said this to me:

"Be a person worth imitating. Imitate people worth being."

I have since tried to discover the origin of that phrase, but so far I haven't been able to. I'm pretty sure McCloud didn't come up with it himself. Doesn't matter.

To this day, I'm not sure why I remembered that statement—but I think I sort of do:

Because it's some of the best advice I've ever been given in my life.

I don't think he had any idea when he said it that it would have made such an impact.

Anyway, I was never able to find out what kind of manager Mike really was, because he was promoted and transferred shortly after I went to work for him, and he died tragically very soon after that.

I do know this:

The staff that had worked with him thought that he was a great manager.

Words to live by?

I think so.

Easier said than done.

1.14 Courtesy And Respect

I didn't come up with the term but I've developed my own acronym for it.

I call it C.R.A.P.

Courtesy-Respect-And-Professionalism.

Or—I guess you could simplify and just say "manners" if you prefer.

Now, you might ask yourself this question:

Didn't you already basically talk about this in the preceding chapters?

Why, yes I did!

Then why are you mentioning it again?

Because, in my experience, even though they might know better, given the right circumstances, managers tend to lose their cool and forget this very important rule:

As a manager, you can never violate the C.R.A.P. rule.

Ever!

Why?

Because if you do, you cannot insist on C.R.A.P. from your staff without looking like a *major hypocrite*.

We were talking about being great, right?

"Well," you might say, "I'm only human. Every once in a while I'm just going to 'lose it' and that's just normal."

AHHHEEEMMM…. Selective rationalization?

Might have been okay when you were on the line, but now that you're a manager, it's not.

Now, you have to be *super-human*.

Perfect 100% of the time.

Remember the 365 rule? This is the same thing.

Here's another reason:

A few chapters from now we're going to discuss personality types and particularly "Amiables."

Amiables simply will not "go" unless you are "nice" to them. And, the minute you're not—*they will never forgive you or ever forget about it*!

We are also going to talk about coaching and counseling. If you are going to coach and counsel someone about his or her own behavior—better if *yours* is beyond reproach.

In fact, unless you want to look stupid—it's critical!

1.15 The Creative Process

Okay, this is another idea I've "stolen" and it's the one *I violate the most*—and it's called the "creative process" or CP for short.

If you want to be the rock in the middle of a shit-storm, master the CP.

If you just want to constantly improve yourself and your operation, master the CP.

Here's the problem:

It's very hard to utilize the CP.

Why?

Most of us are brought up action/results oriented.

We tend to respond *immediately* to almost everything, usually without thinking.

Maybe it's because we don't want to seem *stupid*.

Maybe it's because we want to be the first to answer the

question or solve the problem, so much so that we don't even listen to the question itself, or take the time to properly evaluate exactly what the problem is we are trying to solve.

I blame our grammar school teachers.

Remember the kid in class that always seemed to get his or her hand up first when a question was asked? Then, if the question was answered correctly—and it usually always was—all of the pride and praise that we missed out on because *we* weren't first.

So, rather than *think*, we were conditioned from a very early age simply to *respond*.

Here's how that works:

A question or problem is introduced.

ACTION—we open our mouth before thinking and really do say something stupid.

RESULT—we look stupid.

Then, we do it again, even though it didn't work out so good for us the first time.

Why?

Because, once again, we were *programmed that way.*

Here's the problem:

ACTION/RESULT management doesn't *teach* you anything.

It is a quick two-step process that leads to mistakes *and worse.*

The "creative process," or whatever you want to call it, is a *five-step* way of solving things that works much better. And—here's the good news—with practice it can be implemented just as quickly as the two-step AR process:

STOP

COLLABORATE

ACTION

RESULT

MEASUREMENT

Notice, that ACTION and RESULT are still buried in the list, but the other three additional steps represent a *major difference.*

Let's go back to an example of ACTION/RESULT using the paramedic:

Our paramedic arrives at the scene of an accident. He sees a victim in a wrecked car across the street and jumps out of his van to assist and—boom—gets hit by a truck as he is crossing the road. Our paramedic escapes with minor injuries.

The next week—the same situation arises. Our paramedic does the same thing. Luckily, again, he escapes with minor injuries.

Week after. Our paramedic does same thing again! This time, he gets totally run over.

What happened?

You know the phrase "stop and think."

He didn't *stop* and *think* before taking action the first two times he was confronted with a similar situation, and worse, at the end of each one of them, he didn't "measure" the result.

Let's try the same situation with our paramedic using the CP:

He arrives at the scene of a major accident.

STOP—he stops. Literally. He stops his ambulance and pauses. *This allows him to reset his brain, which will allow him to think more clearly.* Particularly important in a situation where the adrenaline is already flowing.

COLLABORATE—he looks at the physical situation and notices he is across a busy street. Maybe he moves his ambulance, or maybe he just checks traffic before he attempts to cross.

ACTION—he grabs his gear and checks both ways before crossing to help. A speeding motorist passes him before he crosses.

RESULT—this time he doesn't become a casualty himself.

MEASURE—he reminds himself to be careful.

I know the "paramedic" metaphor might be a little goofy, but it's the best one I can think of at the moment.

Anyway, you get the idea.

Here's the point:

When confronted with an issue or a situation, pause for a moment, a day or a week, depending upon the situation (i.e., stop), then think it through and/or enlist the help of others to help you think it through (i.e., collaborate), *then* take action.

Then, once you get a result, make sure to "measure" the result so that the next time something similar happens you can draw upon past experience in order to better deal with the new circumstance in front of you.

Most importantly:

CP allows you to do something AR management doesn't—improve!

Note: for as much as I preach about the CP I still don't use it half the time. I guess I just like looking stupid.

Now, some of you might say that all of the above is just "common sense."

You might say that "people with common sense naturally use some form of the CP" I've just described.

Bingo!

How many people do you actually know like that?

Common sense is the most widely shared commodity in the world, for every man is convinced he is well supplied with it.
—Rene Descartes

1.16 Fear Vs. Panic

I created a separate chapter for this because I think it's *that* important.

Namely, that there is a huge difference between "fear" and "panic" that needs to be pointed out.

Also, it is another paradigm example of how using the Creative Process can assist you in management and in life.

Here's my example:

I have a confession. I used to be afraid of heights.

For instance, when I found myself on say, the sixth floor balcony of a building, there was no way I would lean on the rail.

In fact, I wouldn't even get close to it.

Why then, you might ask, would anyone like that take up the sport of skydiving?

Answer:

Because I thought it might help me get over my fear of heights.

Did it?

No. Only sort of.

By the time I quit the sport, I had done approximately 500 or so successful jumps. I know they were successful because I'm still here.

But… that didn't stop me from being full of fear each time I jumped.

It did, however, stop me from being *panicked* about it.

Here's how:

Obviously, my main fear when I was jumping was that my main parachute wouldn't open.

But, *I had a plan for that eventuality.*

I had a *second* parachute like all good skydivers do and I drilled over and over the procedure for exactly what to do if my first parachute malfunctioned.

Eventually, and more than a couple of times, I actually got

to find out what it was like to have a primary parachute that didn't want to open.

Did I panic?

No.

Was I fearful?

Yes.

But, instead of employing the ole ACTION/RESULT program that probably would have killed me—i.e., panic and do nothing/hit the ground—I used the CP combined with a plan:

Bad parachute—what to do?

Stop (even though I was falling at 120 mph)

Collaborate—Dave, do we have a plan? Why yes we do!

LOOK GRAB LOOK PULL GRAB PULL

Action—execute the plan. Open second parachute.

Result—opened second parachute *and didn't die.*

Measure—since that worked pretty good, make sure to continue to practice and have a plan for a bad parachute.

Moral:

Fear good—might keep you alive.

Panic bad—might even kill you.

Now, some smart aleck might ask:

Well, what if the second parachute hadn't opened?

I would maintain that it would still be better not to panic.

That situation would go like this:

Your second *and last* parachute doesn't work. Yikes!

Stop—even though you are still hurtling towards the earth at 120 mph.

Collaborate—do we have a plan for this? No. Are we going to die? Yes.

Action—enjoy the rest of the way down and ponder how much you've enjoyed being alive. Also, note to self, why was I cheap and didn't buy the best equipment available?

Measure—at least the last few moments of your life were quality moments.

Bonus: no more problems!

Here, once again, is the point:

Just like the paramedic we talked about in the Creative Process, you—as the person in charge—have to be the rock when there is a crisis.

One way is to have a plan.

In fact, *the best way* is to have a plan.

Maybe lots of them.

Have a plan for your family, have a plan for yourself, and have a plan for everyone that you think might be around you in a crisis.

Have a plan for fire. Have a plan for flood. Have a plan for robbery.

In my business, my main concern is not to get anyone killed or seriously injured. So, in order not to be on pins-and-needles about such things, I have a plan and my staff has a plan for virtually any eventuality along those lines:

Fire—we have a plan. We run drills and train all the time for it.

Safety—we have safety meetings. If my staff members have an idea to enhance safety, we usually implement it *even if there is cost involved*. That way, they know I'm *serious* about it!

Other disasters—hurricane, tsunami, earthquake? Yes, we have a written plan and we talk about it all the time.

What if something comes up that you didn't plan for?

This is where the Creative Process and your mastery of it will be most critical.

STOP

COLLABORATE

THEN TAKE ACTION

RESULT

MEASURE

If you live, you probably did a pretty good job of CP.

Anyway, we already discussed the fact that in order to be a

great manager you need to be able to keep a cool head in a crisis.

Fear—as long as there is no outward display on your part—good!

Panic—especially if there is an outward display on your part—bad!

Great managers might indeed be afraid at times, but they don't show it and they never panic.

Never.

1.17 Personality Types

Before, we get started on this topic, let me just say that if I knew where exactly in this book to locate the most important chapters I would do so.

Anyway, this one isn't the *most* important, but it's certainly one of them.

So, let's talk about personality types for a while, because, as mentioned, knowing about them and being able to evaluate them is a critical tool to have in your "great manager" tool box.

Did I say critical?

I meant CRITICAL!

This "personality" thing is not something I came up with. In fact, there are so many variations of the same idea it is hard to pinpoint the original source or I would.

Now, you may have already heard about personality types and you may already be familiar with the basics of how to categorize them, but they warrant review regardless.

In my version there are *four* basic personality types you need to know about:

Drivers

Analyticals

Socials

Amiables

Most people are some combination of *all* of these, but one trait will always be the hands down stand out, the obvious one that best defines an individual's core characteristics.

See if you can spot yourself.

Drivers:

Drivers are action takers, don't much like instruction and are ready for… well… really almost anything that comes their way. They are quick to make decisions and to take action—sometimes to a fault. They generally make good managers, provided that they have someone to keep their feet on the ground.

Ready, fire, aim…

PS—they are usually horrible at the Creative Process until

they make a bunch of bad decisions and painfully learn to use it.

Analyticals:

There is a reason "anal" is imbedded in this word.

Analyticals crave the "facts." Whenever possible, they like to see stuff *written down*. They love S.O.P. manuals and rules in black and white. They love financial forms, written lists, and long reports. Most importantly, they love to go over and over them prior to making a decision on anything—if they ever do.

PS—in general, they make Drivers go nuts. I think of Controllers when I think of Analyticals.

Socials:

Socials are the type of individuals that water seems to run right off of. They rarely hold a grudge and usually remain cheerful despite the circumstances, positive or negative.

They like people and they like hanging around them.

Socials usually make great sales people, because it doesn't hurt their feelings when they get turned down or even if a door gets slammed in their face. In general, they just don't take things personally.

Knock knock.

PS—how do they do it? I want some of their blood!

Amiables

Whooaaa! Watch out!

These are the most "dangerous" of all of the personality types. They are basically the antithesis of Socials though they often hide in Socials "clothing" which sometimes makes them hard to spot.

Amiables usually come off as cheerful individuals on the outside even though on the inside, they might not feel particularly cheerful.

They worry about everything and, in my opinion, are the originators of the saying "waiting for the other shoe to drop."

Personal interaction is not just important to them—*it's critical!* Before any business is discussed, they like to be greeted and acknowledged. No greeting, no communication.

They get their feelings hurt easily and they—like elephants—never forget. NEVER. If you want to know what happened 10 years ago ask an Amiable, especially if it upset them at the time.

Also, Amiables will rarely voice their opinion but they *always have one* and think it's important and expect everyone around them to just "know" what that "very important" opinion is.

Now, in my experience, most people seem to have a dominant personality trait and then a less obvious secondary one from the list above. Oh sure, with any given individual you'll probably find some of all four, but generally one of them will clearly be *primary* and one *secondary*.

For example, I think I am mostly a Driver/Amiable. Certainly, I am not very analytical and not social at all by nature. I'm quick to make decisions and you can hurt my feelings just by looking at me wrong.

Anyway:

From my examples above you can probably figure out which two most apply to you and in which order.

However, it's not only important to understand which category you fall under, but more so, which category *those around you* fall into.

Example:

Remember when we said that at work, your most important customer beside yourself is your boss?

If your boss is a Driver—he/she doesn't want to see your list—he/she just wants you to get it done.

If your boss is an Analytical—he/she is not going to make a move until he/she sees your friggin' list!

If your boss is a Social (not likely, but perhaps)—he/she doesn't give a crap about your list. He/she wants to go to lunch!

If your boss is an Amiable (you poor thing)—he/she wants you to ask about his weekend, his dog, his fish, his kids, his mother and the friggin' weather before you even think about bringing up business.

See what I mean?

Now, let's discuss a few examples using *two* pronounced traits:

Your boss is a Driver/Analytical—he wants to see the list or better yet just to be told quickly what's on it, and he wants whatever is on it done yesterday.

Your boss is an Analytical/Amiable—he definitely wants a hard copy of your list but not, of course, until you've made an appointment to see him. In fact, he'll probably want to discuss it over lunch after you've discussed his dog, etc. Most likely, he'll want to think about your list and anything that requires action for a day, a week, or even a month.

Big difference right?

Here's an example from real life:

When I was a catering director, I once worked with a cranky controller named George.

Now, George was always pretty busy and he wouldn't even look up from his computer when I walked into his office. Until, that is, I figured out that old grumpy George was an off-the-charts Analytical with a handful of Amiable mixed in.

From that point on, I never went to his office without a wad of paper in my hands and a coffee (George loved coffee). It became as if he could see me coming with them.

Anyway, George would drop whatever he was doing, acknowledge me, and ask me what I needed, while he curiously tried to figure out what the papers were that I was holding and whether or not I had remembered to put cream and sugar in his coffee.

Sometimes I would find out what I needed to know and then exit George's office without ever even having shown him the goofy report or financial or whatever I had in my hand.

I did, however, always leave the coffee.

Here's the point:

The quicker you figure out which personality types you are working with the better, especially as it concerns your boss or other managers that may be at your level.

Now, how about the people working for you?

They're Amiables.

All of them.

I can almost guarantee it, unless you manage a bunch of accountant Analyticals or you are standing in the sales office with a bunch of Socials. Otherwise, they are probably Amiables.

Danger.

You better go slow.

You better ask how they are and how their kids are and how their grandma is doing before you ask about the "list" or before you give them an assignment.

Did I say go slow?

I meant—SLOOOOWWW.

As I mentioned, I think I am primarily a Driver with a little bit of dangerous Amiable mixed in. My natural state—since

I am always in a maniacal hurry—is to ignore polite protocols (even though if someone tries that on me I get pissed because of my Amiable side) and to jump right into things.

This *does not work* with Amiables!

Anyway, if you hadn't figured it out before, I am sure by now you might have a pretty good idea of your own primary and secondary traits.

The key is to adapt *your* natural approach to things—i.e., your own primary and/or secondary personality type—and modify them to the personality type to the person in front of you.

In short—you need to "become them" personality wise.

By the way:

Some refer to this as "mirroring and matching," but with the twist that mirroring and matching not only involves mirroring personality, but mannerisms, tone, etc.

Some would take it even further to clothing, styling and more.

Anyway, there are lots and lots of good books that have been written about this—feel free.

Here, once again, is the point:

People tend to like people they are like.

Quiet and thoughtful people generally like quiet and thoughtful people.

Loud people generally like loud people.

Drivers like Drivers.

Etc.

Which reminds me of the next personality type that is *so important* it gets its own chapter.

1.18 Bullies

Originally, I was going to throw "Bullies" on the personality types list as number 5, but upon reflection, I decided that Bullies are *so significant* they deserve their own recognition and their own chapter.

Having said that, feel free to lop that title on the top—or the bottom—of any personality type you run across that warrants it:

Driver/Bully

Amiable/Bully

Bully/Driver/Amiable

Etc.

Here's the thing about bullies:

Bullies are not hard to identify, but they're very hard to "catch."

We probably met our first examples—or, yikes, *became one*

ourselves—early on in school or in some other social circumstance of our youth.

This is the individual that does not seem happy unless they are somehow intimidating others.

There is one caveat to their behavior, however, that is critical to understand. Bullies never bully *up* the social or work hierarchy. In order to function effectively, they must be at least on an "equal" level to the peers they are bullying, or even better, be their superior in some way.

This is when it really gets good for the Bully.

Some parents are Bullies to their kids.

Some cops make great Bullies with the public.

Some teachers with their students certainly—I had a few of those.

Spouses with their spouse—often.

Bosses can be the worst.

Bullies ridicule, torment, belittle, scream, intimidate and sometimes even get physical.

Sometimes they're quiet and stealthy.

Why and how do they get away with it?

They get away with it because *we let them*—plain and simple!

Sometimes, however, for very different reasons:

Sometimes, we're just stuck with them.

Bully for a parent? What's a kid to do? Wait until you're 18 so you can kick their ass?

Mean cop? Probably better just to cooperate.

BUT:

Boss or peer in the *workplace*?

Nope.

No.

No way!

It took me a long time, but here is what I finally discovered about Bullies:

They cannot stand confrontation.

You need to stop them in their tracks.

Sometimes, you might even need to remove yourself from their presence. If you are their inferior you might even have to quit your job. If you are their superior, you need to fire them. If they are your peer, you need to stop them.

How do you stop them?

You confront!

"Zero tolerance" is a term that's getting thrown around a lot these days. How about that?

Example from my youth:

My next-door neighbor was a kid I essentially grew up with—we'll call him "Dan."

Dan was always nice or mean depending on what he was trying to accomplish. When he needed something—nice. When he didn't get it—mean.

Dan was always vacillating between the two extremes so I never really knew what to expect. This is what Bullies are experts at. They suck us in with kindness, then sucker punch us when our guard is down.

Anyway, one day when we were both about 10 or 11 years old, Dan decided to throw a shovel full of dirt on my freshly washed and highly treasured mini-cycle. He did so out of the blue, and seemingly for no reason whatsoever.

Now, I don't know what happened exactly in my head, but that was the limit for me, and Dan seemed to know it. As he took off laughing and running down the street, I somehow produced a large clod of dirt from the pile of dirt he used to throw on my mini.

Call it luck, but I threw that clod *hard* and on target.

Dan was still running, maybe 100 feet away, when that dirt clod found the back of his head and exploded, throwing the otherwise still giggling Bully named Dan on his ass. I'm lucky and Dan was lucky it wasn't a rock or it probably would have killed him.

I followed up that lucky throw by chasing him down and threatening to kick the shit out of him if he ever touched my bike again.

Anyway, Dan never bullied me again. He took a few "test runs," but he never bullied me again.

Here's another from the workplace:

One time, as a catering director, I worked with a Bully Chef we'll call "Sandy."

Now Sandy was a typical bully in that he could either be the nicest guy on the planet or the meanest. In fact, he was nice enough—just enough of the time—that most of the hotel staff sort of liked him, but everyone walked on eggshells around him expecting an "explosion" at any moment.

Note: the general manager of the hotel was fully aware of Sandy's unacceptable behavior—but was having a hard time dealing with it since he had never witnessed any of the behavior himself—which is *typical*. After all, Sandy was always courteous and professional when he was around.

One night, Sandy the Bully Chef decided to explode verbally on one of my banquet captains during a particularly busy evening.

Fortunately, I walked up just in time to witness the entire event. Since we happened to be by the loading dock in the back of the hotel, I offered to have a conversation with Chef Sandy there.

Anyway, as we stepped out of the building and onto the dock, I very "calmly" told Sandy that if I ever saw him treating any of my staff in the manner he had just treated my banquet captain, that I was literally going to kick his ass, and that in fact, I was ready to kick his ass right then and there if he wished.

Now truthfully, I can't speak for my staff. Who knows what kind of subsequent mischief Sandy created.

I can say this: Sandy the Bully Chef never gave me any more unnecessary shit. And, I never received any reports from any of my banquet personnel that he'd given them any more shit either.

I could go on…

Here's the point:

Bullies need to be confronted and dealt with *immediately*.

Here's the problem:

Bullies are excellent at masking their behavior around anyone who can do anything about it—and they are often very good liars.

Around the boss, or any other superior, they are almost always sweet as pie—polite, cordial, helpful, and *very sneaky*.

That is how Bullies get away with bullying so long undetected. They wear a false mask of civility around their superiors, and then secretly torment their peers and/or subordinates when no one else is looking.

Beware.

Which Bullies are the very hardest to spot?

The ones that work for you!

And, unfortunately, sometimes the ones that *live with you.*

Just when the water gets hot around them, Bullies are excellent at cooling things off just before things totally boil over enough to fully expose them. They go into "hiding" until it's safe to re-emerge.

In short, they are clever.

Did I say beware?

Zero tolerance.

If they work for you—sniff them out.

Then, if they don't immediately learn to "fly right"—which in my experience is rare—fire them! Fire them regardless of their otherwise "importance to the operation," regardless of their "tenure," regardless…

Your staff is depending on you!

If you work with one—confront and expose them!

No bullshit!

If you work *for* one—you have some decisions to make.

If you live with one…

1.19 Delegation

Surround yourself with the best people you can find, delegate authority, and don't interfere as long as the policy you've decided upon is being carried out.
—Ronald Reagan

Now we're finally getting down to business!

Let me start by saying this:

I've had a number of managers say to me over the course of my career that they were "just not good delegators."

Either they felt like they wanted to maintain "control" and so it was just "easier" to do the job themselves, or they didn't "trust" someone, or they didn't have the time to train them…

Or….

Or…

Or…

Here's the deal. The very definition of a manager is this:

Manager = Delegator

Definition of a great manager:

Great manager = Master delegator

Period.

For those of you who are tight assed and don't like to "let go," let me ask you this:

If you are going to try to do it all yourself, why have anyone working for you at all?

Even if you work in a very small business—maybe even you and just one employee—*you* should not be doing anything that you hired that other individual to do.

Nothing!

If you are, you are mismanaging!

Example:

Let's say that you're the owner/manager of a small furniture moving business and you have only two employees that do the actual physical moving. Now, only *you* have insurance to drive the truck and you constantly take on projects that require at least three people to do the physical work.

Anyway, *you* personally end up so busy during the day that you cannot even keep up with the bid requests, billing, etc., that are also critical components of keeping your business afloat.

Every day feels like a losing battle.

I have some advice:

Hire another guy!

"I can't afford to hire another guy," is your likely response.

"You can't afford not to," would be mine.

While you are out splitting your gut moving furniture, you're probably losing a ton of business. You're not returning calls promptly and you're not on top of your billing or your payables.

In short, *you are buried.*

Teach someone else to drive the friggin' truck! Get them insurance.

Then, focus on making enough to pay for that extra guy.

When they wreck the truck—which they *will*—fix the truck and turn them loose again.

Here's my point—and I've seen this over and over:

"Managers" who are *too busy* to delegate often find themselves trying to do *everything* and really getting not much of *anything* done—or whatever they are getting done is not getting done very well.

Stop long enough to train your staff, then turn them loose and prepare for mistakes to be made.

Now, let's say you've finally "let go." Let's say that you've trained and assigned one—or one hundred—of your staff to do "stuff."

When should you intervene?

Never!

Well... almost never:

You should only intervene when someone is about to die if you don't. Otherwise, stay out of their way!

Why?

Let me ask you this:

When you have been given something to do, do you want your boss hanging all over you watching you do it?

My experience tells me that once given an assignment, no one appreciates a boss that looms. Worse, a boss that virtually ends up doing the assignment for them.

Now, that's not to say you cannot do follow up or check on progress. In fact, initially you probably should.

Maybe you thought you told your staff to "go left," but whomever you delegated to must have heard "go right," because when you followed up, that is the direction they were going.

Maybe then you should intervene just to save everyone a lot of trouble.

On the other hand, maybe you should go ahead and let them "go right" until they "break something" so they never "go right" again.

Here's the point:

In general, once you have given someone—or a group of "someones"—a task or assignment, you should do everything you can to *hold yourself back from comment* until the assignment is "completed."

Rather than comment "at the moment," make notes (in your

planner?) for the "next time," then discuss those things with your staff prior to the next assignment.

In short, unless someone's life or limb is on the line, or you stand to lose a fortune if you don't speak up, stay out of the way.

Again, make a list as you are quietly observing and bring those points up *later*.

Also, and this is important, try to make sure that when you bring up those points that they are not "stupid" points.

How about an example:

Let's say you have assigned someone to vacuum floors. Let's say when you followed up you discovered that the floors were still dirty. In fact, they were so dirty that you assumed your staffer hadn't even actually vacuumed them!

Here's a suggestion:

Before you criticize them, *make sure that you didn't give them a POS vacuum cleaner to do the job!*

If you *did* give them a POS vacuum and *then make a critical comment*—don't be surprised if they hate you.

Note:

If you couldn't tell, this happened to me, and yes, I hated. I'm over it now, that's why I've forgotten about it. Amiable?

Anyway, at the time, we had such a crappy vacuum cleaner in banquets that there was literally no point in using it—and despite many requests, the GM refused to buy us a new one. Imagine, then, how well received he was when he "commented" that the carpets didn't look very clean in the meeting rooms.

And yes, POS means "Piece-Of-Shit."

Later, when I became a general manager, I made it a point to buy my housekeeping staff new vacuum cleaners at least every couple of years whether we actually needed them or not. After all, I'm paying them all day to friggin' vacuum! Why wouldn't I make sure they are armed with the most awesome vacuum cleaners on the planet?

Example 2:

Once when I was still a catering director we had a visit from some overzealous corporate sales people.

Someone, in all of their corporate wisdom, had decided to put "sales guys" in charge of the catering departments company wide, so of course, the sales guys assumed they had something intelligent to offer about catering, though none of them *had ever worked in catering.*

Now, this was a brand new hotel and so busy in the catering department that we could hardly keep up with incoming calls and requests to book functions. Every day was a struggle for survival just to get back to people so we didn't look like a bunch of unresponsive assholes.

Well… it seems that despite those conditions, the corporate sales guys thought that if we weren't making "outside sales calls," we weren't doing our job.

They insisted that the catering department start making "cold calls," even though I had pointed out to them—or "pushed back" to hear them characterize me—that we already had so much qualified business calling us that we couldn't deal with it as it was.

I suggested that, since we were already so busy, maybe we should take care of *those* customers before we worried about calling people who might or might not want to do business with us.

Anyway, you already know how *that* went over.

Stupid. And yes, we "hated."

Here are a few more observations regarding delegation:

Make sure you are speaking the same "language" as the folks you are delegating to.

Make sure *you know what the heck you are talking about.*

Make sure you have given them the training and the tools—*and I mean really*!

Make sure you have the proper staffing levels—*and I mean really.*

Make sure you are available in case *they* have a question.

Don't ask them to do something—ever—that you wouldn't be willing to do yourself.

Listen to their feedback and if they tell you that the "vacuum" is a POS, buy them a new one!

Above all:

Refrain from input once the assignment has been given.

Rather, make sure you make a note or notes and follow up when the assignment is "complete."

Remember:

If they did it wrong, *it's your fault.* You gave the job to the wrong person. You gave them the "wrong" instructions. Etc.

If they did it right, congratulate them!

Really, you are congratulating yourself for being a good manager!

Note:

I have found that there are about 9 different ways to do something "right" and only about 1 or 2 ways of doing something "wrong"—accidentally killing someone comes to mind.

Anyway, make sure you don't get so dug in on "your" *one* way that you miss a *better* way.

Or, that you are so hung up insisting on *a particular way* of doing something that really, in the big picture, doesn't make the slightest difference, so you end up looking goofy just by insisting on it.

Important point:

Never get between the manager who is responsible for a department and one of his staffers.

As a general manager, I've had this happen often.

It seems innocent enough:

Some lobby attendant, who actually works *for your housekeeper,* asks you where you would like that potted plant located.

Some front office clerk, who actually works *for your front desk manager,* asks you if they can have a new copier.

Or time off.

Or...

Don't do it! *Don't answer the question!*

Turn it around:

"Have you run that past so-and-so (i.e., their *actual* boss)?"

Note: If you're good, you'll whip out your planner and make a note to follow up with your front desk manager regarding the copier—later.

Here's my point—and this is critical if you want to be a master delegator:

Do not get between the manager of a department and one of his staffers.

Period.

Why?

Because when you do, you are inadvertently *subverting the manager you hired to run the department.*

Imagine, as a manager, if you had just told one of your staffers to "go right" and your boss shows up moments later and tells that staffer to "go left."

Why, you might even rightly ask, bother to have the department manager in the first place if you're going to just run everything for them?

I'll guarantee you something:

That is *exactly* what your manager is asking him/herself!

This is one of the biggest faux pas in management and it's done all of the time. Hell, I still do it sometimes!

Don't do it! *Don't do it*!

"How will I know when I've succeeded at delegating?" you ask.

You'll know when the staff in your department, company or small business is doing what you want them to do *basically* the way you'd like them to do it.

"How will I know when I'm great at delegation?"

You'll know that when—besides walking around and encouraging your staff—you personally are not doing *anything* with regard to daily operations *and* your own evaluation is that your department or company is a near 5 (A+) when you *rate* it.

You'll know it when your staff is basically doing everything "exactly" the way you'd like it to be done!

It will be a bonus if your boss/es agree. Heck, you might even get a 5% raise!

"I am just a crappy delegator," you say, "so I guess I will never be a great manager."

How about this:

Find someone who works for you that *is* a great delegator and delegate delegation to *them*!

Patience:

You have to have the "patience of Job" to be a great delegator.

Remember:

"If they were rocket scientists, they'd be rocket scientists."

Just as important:

"If *you* were a rocket scientist, *you'd* be a rocket scientist!"

I've found that a lot of managers expect their staff to have skill levels and even common sense levels that are—if we are honest—way above their pay grade.

Think of this:

Probably they wouldn't be working for you doing the shitty job you've assigned them if they "could do" or "wanted to do" something else more complex at a much higher salary.

Did I say patience?

I meant, *patience*!

Lastly, remember that—next to your boss—your staff members are your most important customers!

Really—just between you and me—they actually are *more important* than your bosses, but that's a discussion for a different day!

Note: I'm no fan of Ronnie Reagan, but his quote regarding delegation is right on the money.

1.20 Management By Walking Around

MBWA isn't a concept that I invented.

Some attribute it to Abe Lincoln and the way he inspected his troops.

Some say it originated in Hewlett-Packard.

We know it is referred to in some of Tom Peters and Robert Waterman's excellent management books of the 1980s.

Here's the point:

It's good practice and it is paramount to becoming a great manager.

Why?

Spontaneous and unplanned trips around your management "sphere" are critical to discovering *what is really going on.*

Don't expect what you don't inspect.

And, it's not enough that you are "cruising" the office or the building or the lot. You need to have purpose.

What is the primary purpose?

Well, there is obviously a big long list that we could easily come up with:

Follow up on projects.

Physical inspection of the premises.

Etc.

But this is the main reason:

To establish relationships with the people working for you!

This cannot be done in your office—*it has to be done in "theirs."*

Remember when we discussed personality types?

What did we decide was the most consistent trait in staff?

They were Amiables!

Regarding that:

Do yourself a favor. When you're out and about MBWA, unless you know for certain that your staffer is a Driver, you would do well to *address them by name* and ask *how they are doing* before barking out a request!

Here's the point:

Particularly if your staff is made up of mostly Amiables—*and it is*—they will not usually volunteer information on the operation *unless you ask.*

Once again, this has to be done in their "office" not yours.

And, you will get a lot more valuable information if you've developed a relationship with them *and they trust you.*

"I don't have time to be out just walking around," you say?

Then you are a crappy delegator.

Fix it.

"I work in a corporate office," you say.

Then get in your car or buy a plane ticket. You should almost *never* be in the corporate office if you have managers and staff working somewhere else.

And, do me a favor when you get there:

Don't stay very long and try not to say anything stupid.

Guilty!

1.21 Pick Your "Things"

Since we were just talking about MBWA, let me make another suggestion:

Pick your "thing" or "things" to always focus on. If you want to call them "hot buttons" go ahead.

Then, make sure your staff knows about them as well.

How will they know?

Because they will hear from you about them all of the time!

Examples:

Nametags—my staff knows that I am *big* on nametags.

Sounds simple, but I will attest to the fact that it is hard to get 100% of my staff to wear them. 99% is easy. 100%? Not so much. But, they know I'm going to ask.

Also, *I'm always wearing mine.* How the heck can I ask them about their nametag if I'm not wearing mine?

Anyway, I figure that if I can't get my staff in nametags then there's not much else I'm going to accomplish with them either.

Names—my staff knows I'm big on the use of names.

I attempt never to pass one of my staff without using their name.

I once managed a 4 star hotel where the elevator to the lobby emptied literally right in front of the front desk. My staff at that hotel was charged with facially recognizing whomever the guest was that was getting on or off the elevator and greeting them by name.

They got damn good at it, I'll say that.

Neatness—my staff knows I'm a neat freak.

My office is neat. My personal vehicles are always spotless. Since I have also had the opportunity to have many of them in my home, they know that too is kept spotless.

This has made *my staff* neat freaks.

When something is in disarray, they know I'm going to ask WTF.

It's rare. They take a lot of pride in not having to answer that question.

Anyway, I could go on. There are probably twenty or thirty "things" that my staff knows I'm going to focus on if it's not right.

Here's the point:

Focusing on a few specific things all of the time will let your staff know you are *paying attention all of the time.*

Focusing on a few things *specific to your staff* will let them know that you are *paying attention to them.*

Disclaimer: you will hear me say a lot about not interfering or getting between staff and management—but my managers know that regarding my "things" I will intervene *on the spot if I see something amiss*—and I've forewarned them.

I will also make a point of letting my managers know later that I did so—usually much to their chagrin.

1.22 Decision Making

In any moment of decision, the best thing you can do is the right thing, the next best thing is the wrong thing, and the worst thing you can do is nothing.

—*Theodore Roosevelt*

Remember when I made the claim that the very definition of a manager is "delegator"?

Same thing with decision making:

Manager = Decision maker

Great manager = Excellent decision maker.

I've worked both for and with managers who couldn't make a decision to save their own life, and I've worked with managers who could make decisions right away, but they were often "bad" ones.

Here's where the personality "types" really come into play:

Drivers—love to make decisions and often become managers just so they can do so. Ready, fire, aim!

Socials—they would rather someone else make the decisions, but are excellent at carrying them out once made.

Analyticals—they'll eventually make a decision given enough time and the proper paper work to back them up, but the house might have already burned down by then.

Amiables—they prefer not to make a decision about anything. That is not what they are paid to do damn it. But, they will be happy to secretly criticize any decision anyone else makes, confident that their decision would have been better.

As you might have surmised, the descriptions above virtually rule out Socials and Amiables as ready and able decision makers.

That leaves us with really only two potential personality types as managers really capable and willing to make decisions:

Drivers or—God save us—Analyticals!

The problem with Drivers as bosses is that they often jump to conclusions too quickly and are prone to making bad decisions as a result.

The problem with Analyticals as bosses is that they never seem to come to a conclusion or take an excruciating amount of time doing so.

Here's my point:

If you want to be a great manager, regardless of your dominant personality type, you are going to need to be able to "morph" yourself into nice combination of both Driver and Analytical.

Drivers need to remember the CP and use it! I have never known a great Driver manager who didn't have several Analyticals on their team assisting them in that process.

Analyticals need to remember that we are all going to die someday—so make a friggin' call! I have never known a great Analytical manager who hadn't reached the same conclusion, and kept a Driver or two around them to force the issue.

What about if you know yourself to be predominately Social or Amiable? Can you still become a great manager?

Yes, of course.

But…

Only if you are able to "morph" yourself into a well-balanced Driver/Analytical when it's decision time.

And… as a manager…

It's almost *always* decision time!

Danger!

Here are the three major exceptions to "decision time":

First exception:

It is *not* decision time when the decision in question *should be made by your boss*—not you!

Don't take the bait.

Ask yourself if it's "your call" or "the boss's." If it's your boss's call or should be—force him/her to make it.

Note: I like to get those types of decisions memorialized in writing, initialed, or confirmed by email—especially ones I don't necessarily agree with—in case "someone" has a memory problem later!

Second exception:

It is definitely *not* decision time if the decision in question *should be made by one of your staff.*

That's not to say that you can't advise them when they ask for assistance, but you should *insist that they make the call.*

Third exception:

Don't make any decision that thwarts your own chain of command.

Remember the "rules" of effective delegation?

Example—again:

Let's say one of your line staffers asks you where to "put the plant in the lobby."

The incorrect reply is "over there."

The correct reply is "check with your supervisor" or "did you ask your supervisor?"

Note: As mentioned before, this is one of the hardest "rules" not to break, especially if you like to make decisions. Don't do it! You might think you're being helpful when you are really just undermining the authority of one of your managers or supervisors. If you don't like where the plant ended up, tell the *manager you put in charge of that area*!

1.23 Training

I'm only including a chapter on this topic so that no one will cry about me leaving it out.

Training?

Yes, of course!

Train, train and then train some more!

Run a firehouse?

Show your new fireman where the hose bibs are.

Run a hospital?

Show your new neurosurgeon where the light switch is in the operating room and the drawer where the scalpels are kept.

A platoon?

A demonstration regarding the proper operation of an AR-15 is in order.

And… Of course…

Please show *everyone* where the restroom is!

Regarding training, I will say this:

My sense is that it is the "line" guys in any operation who probably get the best training because they get *most of their training from their peers.*

Managers?

Sexual harassment and how to avoid a union run.

That's it.

You're ready.

Sink or swim baby!

PS—those of you who are already managers? Tell me I'm wrong!

1.24 Communication

"It's not what you say, but *how* you say it."

Truer words were never spoken, right?

Especially as it concerns *Amiables*!

Anyway, I'm not going to spend a lot of time boring you about the necessity of becoming a good communicator in order to become a great manager. We just talked about it regarding delegating.

And, there are plenty of quick studies of the "dos" and "don'ts" out there that you can study and practice mastering—and they're probably much better than anything I could come up with here.

But…

From experience, here is a word of caution:

Don't ever assume that anything you say by word or email or text or memo will be received the way you intended.

There is a great Far Side comic from years ago that almost everyone has seen at one point or another that illustrates this point.

It is called "Things you say to your dog" and it goes like this:

THINGS YOU SAY TO YOUR DOG

> Okay, Ginger! I've had it! You stay out of the garbage! Understand, Ginger? Stay out of the garbage or else!

WHAT YOUR DOG HEARS

> Blah, Ginger! Blah, blah, blah! Blah, Ginger? Blah!

The question I often ask myself is this:

Why is everybody going "right" when I thought I *specifically* told them to go "left"?

If you find yourself often asking the same sort of question, especially as it pertains to delegation, then your instructions or the way you are delivering them sucks and you need to fix it.

That, or you simply have the wrong person in the job.

Remember "It's your fault…" ?

Exactly.

Fix it.

If something isn't being done the way you want it done, then something is wrong on *your end*. This would be an excellent time to utilize the Creative Process to figure out why.

Maybe you are speaking English and your audience only speaks Spanish.

Maybe you just said it when you should have written it down.

Maybe you have the wrong person in the job.

Maybe you barked out an order to an Amiable without saying "hello" first.

Maybe you have the wrong boss.

Whatever the problem is, it's on *you* to figure it out.

Just a reminder:

In person, something like 50% of the "message" you are sending is based on how you look, 40% is your tone of voice and facial expression, and only 10% is what you are actually saying.

In texts or email:

Think about them 3 times before sending. Who is your audience? Driver: short and to the point. Analytical: report attached. Social: make a date for lunch. Amiable: ask them how they are before you ask anything else.

Notes:

Write them by hand! *Write them by hand*!

Especially if they are personal, congratulatory or thank you notes.

Did I say write them by hand?

Names:

Use them often. Like "Ginger," people *love* to hear their name.

Did I say love?

I meant *love*!

Especially Amiables.

Who's an Amiable?

Almost everyone!

1.25 Coaching and Counseling

Remember when I was talking about your own personal behavior earlier on?

Remember when I suggested that you *must* behave?

Remember when I said that you have to be the shining example of whatever you expect your staff to become?

Remember when I said you must "never"…

Now, we're going to find out why.

Let's say you have a problem with someone being late all of the time.

Let's say you have a problem with someone "harassing" someone.

Let's say you have a problem with someone's:

Temper

Attendance

Appearance

Cleanliness

Follow through or lack thereof

Lying

Cheating

Stealing

Drinking problem

Etc.

Are you really going to sit down and talk to one of your staff members about problems with any or all of the above when *you* are the poster child of that kind of behavior?

Would you like to have the edge in this type of conversation?

Yes?

Then you personally need to be the squeaky-est clean-est person in the friggin' building!

This means you haven't just been "good" for a while. This means you have been "good" 365 days a year—*every day, month and year you've been wherever you are!*

Why?

Because otherwise, you'll look like an idiot!

Worse, you will look like a complete hypocrite!

They know what you've done!

Is that any way to start a coaching and counseling session?

I think not!

In fact, don't even bother.

Resign.

You are the one who needs counseling!

On the other hand, let's say you *are* squeaky clean.

Congratulations! *You are one in a thousand.*

Now, you can start talking!

Here are some pointers and some "do" and "do nots." These all seem obvious, but bear repeating:

Do not do any negative coaching in front of anyone's peers. You can however, if necessary, have another manager or superior involved. In fact, if it is a touchy situation, I wouldn't have one *without* another manager or HR director in the room.

Do not make it about the individual. Make it always about their behavior.

Make sure you have specifics.

Example:

"Late all of the time" doesn't cut it.

Which day/date and exactly how late with a wad of notes on your desk beside you to back you up.

Whatever you are counseling—*the more specific the better.*

I've made the mistake of attempting such things without my "ducks" in a row and had my ass handed to me by the staffer I was counseling.

"When was I late?"

"Ah... well... err... you're just late a lot..." is not a good answer.

Make sure you *hear the staffer out* and get the whole story from their side.

Example:

"I was late because my mother had a stroke and I had to take her to the hospital" is a way different answer than "I was late just because I was late."

Make sure you get "both sides" of the story either before or during the counseling! Don't jump to conclusions.

This is critical! I am guilty of not doing this and if you are not careful, you will be too!

Example:

Let's say you don't particularly "like" a specific staffer for whatever reason.

Let's say you heard said staffer hit another staffer in the break room.

You are ready to fire him instantly, right?

Except, what you find out—*because you are a great manager and because you endeavored to find out both sides of the story*—is that the staffer not only didn't hit another staffer, the other staffer actually hit *him*.

Here's the point:

Don't jump to conclusions. If you're a Driver, Amiable or even Social you are likely to.

Get both sides, or three sides, or *four* sides to the story if necessary before you take action.

Lastly:

You need to develop good listening skills!

Confession time:

I am generally *a terrible listener*! Since I am completely self-obsessed, I really only like to hear myself speak.

In order for me to have a chance to hear anyone, I have to *remember* that I am a terrible listener and *force* myself to be a good one.

Also, it's very hard to be a good listener when you have already come to a conclusion about something or you have already formed a hard opinion. Do your best to hang on to an "open mind."

In general:

Counseling time = Creative process time!

1.26 Documentation

By "documentation"—I mean mostly as it pertains to your staff:

Less is more.

Okay, I'll admit it. I used to think the opposite.

And, by the way, in a union house, I still would.

In a union situation, if someone is "one minute late" you have to document the tardiness or the next "member" will cry foul when he's 10 minutes late.

Now, I'm not "for" or "against" unions per se. In fact, I think overall, that unions have directly or indirectly inspired some admirable behavior from companies whose behavior otherwise might not have been so admirable.

My "problem" with unions, if I have one, is that they seem to operate by the theory that they can only survive by constantly sowing seeds of discontent and/or malcontent among their members towards management.

I've worked in both kinds of houses, and I prefer non-union, especially in hospitality.

For the purpose of the rest of this conversation, let's assume you are working in a non-union environment. It's just so much easier.

Anyway, as I mentioned, I used to think documentation was a "more the merrier" proposition.

Annual performance reviews.

Write ups (and the threat of them) for every infraction.

Etc.

Now?

Not so much.

Why?

Mainly because less paper is less to hand over when someone sues you!

And, they will sue you! At least someone will at one point or another.

My experience with mandatory performance reviews is that they are rarely well done and are not necessary to motivate someone anyway. Your staff should always know where they stand and how they are doing simply *because you've told them so, and often*!

When I allow someone to be "written up" now, it means that they are on the road to being terminated.

I am very consistent about that.

In short, *consistency* is the key regarding documentation.

Whatever you do, *do it consistently.*

How about this idea?

Get so good at hiring and so good at motivating that you hardly ever have someone working for you that you "need" to document?

How about that?

Here's what you should document:

Whenever your boss approves or asks you to do something that might need to be "remembered" in the future.

"I didn't approve that raise!"

Yes sir, you did. Here are your initials.

"I didn't approve that purchase."

Ahh... err... yes sir, you did. Attached is the email.

Anyway, I am far more prone to documenting things that my bosses ask me to do than documenting anything regarding my staff.

You get the idea.

CYA!

1.27 Firing Someone

Firing someone is probably number two on the list of least liked aspects of being a manager, superseded only by public speaking.

It doesn't have to be. In fact, I've found it can actually be quite enjoyable—particularly if the staff member *deserves* to be fired!

Most managers—including me—often wait way too long to fire staff members *who should be fired.*

Do it!

Fire them!

If you know they *should be fired*—fire them!

Important:

Don't let the lack of documentation or the fact that they are "really nice" or that you are "really nice" or that your company counsel wants more "cause" before said counselor is "comfortable."

Fun fact:

Lawyers are *never* comfortable with terminations!

It's okay. They are there to pick up the pieces when you and your company get sued for not following their sage advice!

"That's easy for you to say, but I work in a union shop. I can't fire them without a boatload of documentation."

Fire them! It will take more effort on your part, but it can be done. Start loading the boat.

Here's the thing:

Do you want to be a great manager?

Great managers run great operations.

You cannot have a great operation without great staff members, can you?

Figure it out.

Fire them!

Conversely:

Some managers fire people for questionable reasons before considering just "who" exactly they will get to replace the individual they are firing!

For example:

If you are considering firing Freddie for screwing up the "rocket formula," maybe you should also consider—based on the amount of money you are paying, the market conditions for employment, etc.—just who in the heck you are going to get to replace Freddie.

Also, in my experience, it's a lot more likely that Freddie just followed *your* recipe!

Watch out for that.

Remember the "it's your fault" thing?

Here's my point:

I've watched bosses and managers fire people for dubious reasons, only to discover that the replacements they found were *worse*—or, in some cases, that they had trouble finding replacements at all.

Firing time = Creative Process time!

Once you have made the decision to fire someone remember these things:

The person is a human being!

You should stress that the termination is about their job performance, not them as an individual.

The actual firing should *never involve a long conversation.* If it goes beyond a minute or two you have made a mistake.

Make sure you are in a position to pay them and collect anything necessary from them such as keys, etc.

Have someone with you to witness, preferably your HR manager or someone else higher in management than the person you are firing.

Wish them well—*and mean it.*

1.28 Public Speaking

Tell 'em what you're gonna tell 'em...

Tell 'em...

Then, tell 'em what you just told them...

And, make them laugh and cry in the process...

That, my friends, is the recipe for a good speech. Perhaps for a great one!

Now, I have to admit, I would rather have a rectal exam than speak in public. By "public," I mean any group of more than a couple of people.

I'm not alone. Google says at least 3 out of 4 people feel the same way:

Glossophobia—fear of public speaking. Somehow related to the Greek word for "tongue."

Go figure.

Anyway, you'll never be a great manager without becoming at least a very good public speaker.

Already have that down?

Good for you!

If not, you need to.

How?

Practice. Get help. Take a class.

Toastmasters?

I was fortunate enough to take a couple of PS courses in college. One thing that probably helped me the most was that the instructor liked to give us a speaking topic and then he would *video record it* as we delivered it.

Now, I used to think I was on the verge of either passing out or puking when I was giving those speeches way back then, but, when I would watch the playback, I noticed something critical:

I couldn't tell.

I wasn't obviously sweating and my voice wasn't wavering. In fact, I actually looked pretty calm.

Anyway, barring a membership to Toastmasters, here is a suggestion:

The next time you have to give a speech of any kind, make sure someone video records it for you. Then, play it back and see how you did and how you actually looked when you were delivering it.

You'll be surprised that you "appear" much calmer than you probably felt at the time, which will give you more confidence the "next" time.

Obviously, preparation, practice, and determining exactly "who" your audience is will also be major factors in how you perform.

On that note, don't forget personality types:

If you're speaking to a group primarily of Drivers—don't begin by telling them about your dog.

If it's a group of Analyticals—make sure you have charts, graphs and handouts.

If it's a group of Amiables—do tell them about your dog and *ask them about theirs*!

If it's Socials—make sure it includes lunch and an open bar!

Note: especially in large groups, I always assume that most of the folks are Amiables. In my view, it's a safe-than-sorry strategy, because in my experience, most people are Amiables or at least that is number 2 in their personality profile.

Lastly, try not to lie. It's hard to give a good speech when what you are saying is bullshit and you know that it's bullshit.

Scratch that... How about this?

Don't lie.

Easier.

1.29 Writing Skills

This is another topic that seems so obvious that it shouldn't bear mentioning. However, mastering the art of writing in some sort of coherent fashion has not been the norm of my experience with most managers.

In fact, I've known some managers that were pretty high up in the corporate ladder that didn't seem to know the difference between a subject and a predicate.

Personally, although one of my degrees is in English Literature, I don't really know the difference between a subject and a predicate either.

What I do know is what sounds right and what doesn't. I credit that "skill" mostly to my prolific reading habits. I've always read a lot and written a lot.

Spelling? Not so much. But now with the advent of spell check and the other magnificent tools that inhabit any good word processing application, I have been mostly saved.

Of course, thanks to the many idiosyncrasies of the English language, one still needs to know the difference between such things as "their" and "there" or "its" and "it's," and my favorite, "meet" and "meat," so spell check isn't the end all. Beware.

Tips:

Read whatever you've written *out loud*. If it doesn't sound right, it's probably not right.

If in doubt, have someone proofread your work.

Here's my point:

If you are a manager, you are going to have to *write things*. If you want to be a good manager, you will need to be a good writer. If you want to be great, you'll need to be a *very* good writer.

Practice.

Or…

Find someone on your staff that *is* a great writer…

And…

Yes!

Delegate!

1.30 Meetings

Let me be brief:

Let your meetings be brief. In fact, *insist* that your meetings are brief. No one, including you, has the time to sit in a meeting. *You* should be out MBWA!

One hour. Not a minute more. Regardless of the topic or the number of attendees.

That's my rule for meetings. I'm not saying it's anyone else's, but it should be.

Did I say one hour? I meant 60 minutes.

And that also means *starting them exactly when you say you will.*

I had a general manager that worked for me once that wouldn't let his staff into the room if they were even one minute late for one of his meetings! At one minute past "whatever," he would lock the door and force whoever the unfortunate and tardy individual was to have a very uncomfortable private briefing *later* of what was covered.

Did I say I loved that GM? Oh yes! Still do!

Where were we?

Oh yeah—one hour!

Unless, of course, *the meeting can be done in less time than that*!

Anything longer is a "class" or a "seminar." If you are planning on conducting a class, or a seminar, a conference, symposium, or whatever, *then call it that*!

Filibuster?

Otherwise:

One hour—maximum. Less than one hour if possible. 15 minutes? Better!

And:

Start *exactly* on time no matter *who has or hasn't shown up.*

Stick to the agenda. Don't ever "back up" because you let someone in late.

Don't let "that guy/gal" commandeer your meeting—shut him/her down. Nicely if possible, but shut him/her down!

Sidebar later?

"Pow-wow" later?

End the meeting *before* or *exactly when* you said you would.

Not five minutes later. Not ten!

Want to make your meetings really short?

Have everyone stand for them. No chairs.

Woo hoo!

Here's my point:

When you are engaged in having regular meetings and your staff knows what to expect and exactly how long to expect it, *they will be far more attentive.* Also, they might think that *you actually know what you are doing.*

"Well," you might ask, "what if I have way more than an hour's worth of stuff to cover?"

Answer:

Either break your agenda up into as many one hour meetings as you need or turn it into a class and call it a "class" or "boring waste of time" or whatever you want to call it—just don't call it a "meeting."

Better yet, yank all of the bullshit out of your agenda that is making your meeting turn into a "class" and turn it back into a one hour meeting!

Did I say never go over one hour?

Also critical:

Make sure the discussion points of your meeting pertain to *everyone in the meeting*!

Example:

Make sure that your Chef doesn't have to sit and listen to an issue you are having at the front desk! *This is one of the most often made mistakes*!

Lastly:

All of the above only works if you never fail to show up on time yourself.

Did I say never?

Guilty.

But rarely—and, usually only if I would have to "kill" someone to get them out of my face so I could be on time.

1.31 Planners

Speaking of staying on track and being on time, what kind of a "planner" do you use?

You do know that it is *critical* that you have one, right?

More critical is that you *use it*! I know a lot of people that have these amazing planners that forget to read them or use them at all!

Heck, even Santa has one:

"He's making a list, and checking it twice…"

Sorry.

I still use a good old-fashioned "Day-Timer" myself, but maybe you are more "with it" and have figured out how to do things completely electronically.

I don't really care "how" you do it, as long as you do!

Why?

I don't know about you, but I only remember my ex-girlfriends, my wife's birthday and our anniversary. Otherwise, half of the time, I am not certain what day it is without looking in my planner.

Now, since I am half way "with it," I sometimes use Siri as a "parachute," just in case I really need to make sure I don't miss something. More about "parachutes" later.

I also set alarms on my phone.

Anyway, unless you have a photographic memory and an uncanny ability to call things back into your consciousness just at the right moment, *you must develop your skills with some sort of planner.*

Here are just some of the ways I use mine:

I write down important meetings on the date they are going to occur and a note the day prior reminding me about the meeting.

I write down assignments my boss has given me and make notes before and on the date the assignment is due.

I write down assignments I've given my staff and when they are due so I can follow up on them to see that the assignments in question are actually done!

I make lists of meeting topics that *should be discussed later* rather than at the moment that I think of them.

I make lists of people I need to call and when to call them.

I write down goals.

I write down birthdays, anniversaries, graduations, and milestones.

I write down "thank you" notes or "thank you" calls that need to be made.

Really, I write down anything that I want to *actually happen*. Critically, I write them down *the moment I think of them* so I don't forget them!

Then—and here is the even more critical part—I *review* my list daily and even sometimes hourly to make sure I haven't missed anything.

If something or some goal still needs to happen that didn't, I move it further down the line in my planner—but I never let it go or cross it off *until it's done* or it has lost its priority completely.

Some people have accused me of being efficient.

No, I've just become really good at using a planner.

While we're on this topic let's just talk a second about trace systems:

Once again, unless you are Albert Einstein and you have an internal alarm that will go off whenever you "set" it, *you need a trace system* to back up your planner.

Example:

Your boss asks you to do something on a certain day a month from now.

How are you going to remember without "tracing" it so a month from now you are reminded to do it?

You need to order something critical to your operation, but it's too early now—you really need to order it in three months.

How are you going to remember?

I cannot tell you how many very "good" managers I've encountered who otherwise would have been "great" had they developed good habits with the use of a planner and also maintained a very good trace system.

"Oh man, sorry I forgot."

Ugh!

If it helps, use your planner like everyone now uses their goofy cell phone—checking it every few minutes or so like they're hoping to find out if they've just won some cosmic lottery or are on the verge of discovering the meaning of life. Just try not to do it while you're driving!

1.32 Goals Lists

I don't know about you, but even with a good planner, sometimes I have a tough time staying focused.

I started writing my "goals" down when I heard or read about the fact that most highly successful people keep (or kept) their goals written down and close at hand.

So, one page in the back of my Day-Timer is a short-term goals list and one page is a long-term goals list. Usually one year vs. five years or something like that. I combine work goals with personal goals just because I find it easier.

December has become sort of my ritual month to set my one-year goals list and to update my five.

Here is a "short" version of my current one-year goals on the personal side:

Finish management book

Buy a fast car

Quit smoking—no hurry

Take wife on fantastic trip

Save X dollars

Anyway, it still sort of shocks me when I ask people about their own goals lists only to find out that *they don't have one.*

Do what you want.

But, don't be surprised if the years go by and you suddenly realize that you haven't accomplished much.

Also:

Nothing will give you as much satisfaction as putting a big check mark next to one of the items on your list that you have actually achieved—especially the "big" personal ones.

In addition to my written goals lists, I also copy a lot of them down in my planner. Sometimes, it might just be notes about things that will help me actually achieve the ultimate goal.

Example:

If I want to take a big trip, in addition to writing it down on my goals list, I'll also write down "plan the big trip" the appropriate amount of months before the trip in my planner to make sure *I book the trip.*

Won't happen if you don't book it.

If I want to have a certain amount of money by the end of the year, I'll make a note monthly about how much I need to bag and by when to get to the goal.

Won't happen if I wait until the end of the year.

If I want to write a book by year-end, I make a note in my planner to work on it and move said note each week in my planner until it's done.

Maybe book will happen. For sure it won't happen if I don't constantly work on it.

Anyway, so much for the "highly successful" part of the goals thing.

Ugh. I'm still waiting for that to happen.

But, I do manage to achieve a bunch of the goals I set, and I think a big part of that is simply having them *written down*.

1.33 Now

Now is the time, the time is *now*!

Okay, I admit it, I think of myself as one of the greatest procrastinators of all time.

I like to put shit off. Especially things *I don't want to do.*

Secretly:

I think I'm lazy.

For example:

Writing. I have put off writing this book for years. The idea of actually sitting down and writing makes my butt pucker.

Budgets.

Doing my tax return.

Cleaning out the _____.

Balancing my checkbook.

Etc.

Etc.

I'm sure we all have long lists of things we like to put off.

Worse, are things we *should do* but *never do* because we simply forget all about them or we say we are or were just "too busy".

Ugh!

Think you can be a great manager by operating that way?

This is what I've found:

If it's possible to do it now—do it now!

Return the phone call.

Return the email.

Finish the budget.

Walk around the property.

Have the meeting.

Fire them!

Not later. *Now!*

And, most importantly, if it's not possible or advisable to do it "now," *write whatever it is down* somewhere and do it as soon *as it's possible to do it.*

Use of a planner? Start one now!

Goals list? Write one now!

Remember when we discussed "most important customer" at work?

Your boss, right?

Especially, when your boss asks you to do something—*do it now!*

Can't do "it" now?

Write it down in your planner—then do it ASAP.

He or she might just get the idea that you are pretty efficient.

In fact, so many managers in my experience *fail to do this* that your boss might just get the idea that you are *the most efficient person that has ever worked for them*!

Conversely, your staff might get the same impression.

In fact, since you are the one setting the example of efficiency—you might just be able to demand the same from them without looking like an asshole.

Now!

Now!

Now!

And if it can't be now, then for God's sake, make sure it's done as soon as it's possible to do it.

Lastly:

When someone asks me to do something, I like to report back to "them" that the task is done whenever it finally gets done without that "someone" having to ask me—*especially if that person is my boss.*

If the particular task is going to take some time, I like to *periodically update* so whoever it is doesn't think I spaced it—*especially if that person is my boss.*

With my staff:

I train them to operate the same way.

In fact, many of them have become so good at the "now" thing that they are actually better at it than me!

Guess what?

Some people have accused my staff members of being extremely efficient!

Does that make me smile?

Why, yes it does.

So:

When is a good time?

Now!

And, on the chance that "now" isn't the right time, then make sure whatever the task is, it's done as soon as it can reasonably be done—and report!

Once again—for me—without a planner tucked under my arm and constant reference to it, coupled with a goals list and a good trace system, nothing would ever happen.

1.34 Organization

Or:

A place for everything and everything in its F-ing place.

Or:

Neat and clean as a whistle.

Some people—including myself—have accused me of having obsessive-compulsive disorder.

Now, I know some people actually do have that affliction to the point where it is ruinous of their lives and I am not trying to make fun of that. Mine is mild comparatively—I just insist on "neatness."

I think neatness is something in your genes, but maybe part of my "obsession" with it is because I grew up in a home with a working mom and three siblings. Suffice it to say, our home was rarely what you could call "neat," but somehow, in the midst of my upbringing, I became a neat-nick.

Fun fact:

Two of my favorite things to do are to vacuum something with a great vacuum cleaner and/or to hose something off, preferably with a high powered nozzle and lots of water pressure!

Other examples of my obsessive nature:

No "clutter." I don't like "stuff" or lots of "objects" spread around willy-nilly.

My cars—clean.

My closet—organized.

My lawn—freshly mowed.

My shirts—pressed.

My hotel—immaculate—at least as far as anyone could reasonably see.

On the other hand:

Behind the doors of a cupboard?

I'll sometimes let things slide.

Kitchen pantry?

Ugh! Out of date! Out of date!

My sock drawer?

Not always so good.

But, at least on the surface, *neat and clean*!

Here's my point:

Unfortunately for the "slobs" of the world, the bulk of the population that they will run into professionally seem to highly value "neatness."

Heck, even the "slobs" that I know highly value neatness even if they are unwilling to be neat themselves.

Anyway, you can "selectively rationalize" that you are a "comfortable slob" all you want—but you won't be great as a manager.

Period.

1.35 Work Ethic

Never work one second more than you need to.
           –Frazier

Here's one thing I finally figured out:

When I'm on my death bed, I don't think I'm going to suddenly sit up and say I wished that I'd worked more!

By the way, for those of you who haven't had the pleasure of leaving a company by being fired or even leaving of your own accord, let me say this:

Even after years, or decades, or a lifetime of dedication, loyalty, commitment and busting your ass—unless you work for me, *maybe*—no one is going to give a shit when you finally do leave.

In fact, human resources will be so concerned with getting your company ID and your keys back it'll make your head swim.

In fact, it might just be one of the most disappointing moments in your life.

If you manage to *die* while working somewhere:

There will be a short, and perhaps somewhat sympathetic email sent out, saying what a "great" person you were, that nicely transitions into "redirecting instructions" regarding your emails to someone else in the company *who isn't dead yet!*

That's it!

I'm not saying that it's bad. I'm just saying that is the way it is.

I'm saying it so that you put work in the proper perspective and *give it the weight it deserves.*

Anyway, as a manager, here's my formula for how much you need to work:

Until the job gets "done."

Better yet:

Until the job gets "done" to the extent that it needs to get done, given the fact that no one is going to give a shit how it was done a decade from now, probably even a year from now, a month, or maybe even a day.

Having said all of that, that doesn't mean you can't be a badass at what you do.

It doesn't mean that you can't be super productive, super loyal or even super valuable.

And, it doesn't mean that you won't have to work 80 hours a week in order to accomplish it!

What it does mean is that you must learn to be extremely efficient with your use of time.

What it does mean is that *you* have to be the one who "gives a shit" as a matter of *your own personal pride*.

When I first started in the hospitality business, I thought being at work 60-70 hours a week and basically killing myself was the right thing to do.

Now, I think that if I even *need* to "show up" I've mismanaged something.

Here is my work formula now:

At the start of the day, I imagine that I've just flipped over an hourglass and that the sand has started running. Then, I go head down and butt up to get accomplished what needs to be accomplished in order to make me look like a super efficient badass manager.

Generally, I get more done than many of my peers because I concentrate on the basics first and don't let myself get mired in distractions.

Anyone tries to hand me something?

My first thought is how can I either eliminate the task completely or to *delegate it*.

Why?

Because I want to go home.

Remember our discussion about "most important customer?"

And, even more importantly, I want anyone around me—especially my bosses—to wonder how the hell I get so much accomplished.

Here's my point:

If you are a manager and you are working 80 hours a week, then you are either:

Brand new at the job and you *need* to be there! Okay.

Completely disorganized. Not okay.

Have trouble with priorities. Not okay.

Are almost certainly crappy at delegation. Double not okay.

Are so insecure that you feel you have to be at work all time. Triple not okay.

As a manager you should *only* be doing the following:

Working on things that are *going to happen in the future.* If you are doing anything that involves day-to-day ops besides dealing with some sort of crisis du jour, you are probably mismanaging.

Following up on anything you have delegated. This is critical. For as lovely as my staff is, they will not necessarily get things done unless I follow up.

Maintaining relationships MBWA! In other words, finding out what is really going on.

Taking care of your boss.

Note:

Some bosses think that unless you are at work a million hours a week and have your hands in "everything" you are not doing your job.

My opinion is that if your department is not running like a proverbial Swiss watch you are not doing your job, and how much "time" you spend doing or not doing it is irrelevant.

Hint: If your department *is* running like a Swiss watch and your boss is critical—offer to spend some time with him/her on their own *delegation skills*!

Or... not.

1.36 Financials/Controllers

Ugh!

Okay, I guess we need to talk about this.

I admit it—*I hate accounting*. On any given day I couldn't explain the difference between a debit and a credit. In fact, I secretly think you have to be a little bit weird to even want to know.

Having said that, there are some things you *must* know about accounting and financial reports that are important:

First, businesses run on them!

I guess we're stuck.

If you're a manager, the financial report that pertains to your department or business or whatever is really the only measurement tool that anyone is going to pay attention to, so you'd better understand it.

Here's my point:

Even if you cannot stand to deal with the "numbers"—i.e., you're a Driver, Social or an Amiable—you absolutely need to devote enough time with them to learn to be "dangerous."

Learn to read the reports and develop at least a basic idea of how they are produced and who produces them.

There is a part of me that, even today, wishes I had done a stint in accounting long enough to be able to pull a hotel financial report myself. I might have blown my own brains out in the process—but still.

Also—and this is big—you need to be aware of the fact that financials are only *as good as the numbers that are used to create them*. In short, financials can be misleading or flat out *wrong*.

Learn to question them!

Now, a short word about Controllers.

We need them!

We need them in their offices *counting*.

We do not need them running anything or doing anything else! They're Analyticals!

You know those obnoxious charges the airlines charge for extra baggage that makes you absolutely hate them?

I am going to guarantee you this: Controllers came up with that idea!

You know the "codes" you were given that you can never remember in order to make copies because "too many" copies were being made?

Controllers.

Forms? Fill out this and fill out that?

Controllers.

Now, you may think from what I've just said that I'm "down" on controllers.

Nope.

In fact, just the opposite.

I love them because they—most of them—learned to *count*!

We need them to count shit so we can figure out where we need to go next management wise.

Lastly:

There is nothing worse than a bad controller and nothing

better than a really good one—and there is no better way to find out than *a good audit*!

Did I say audit?

I meant AUDIT!!!

1.37 False Comparisons

All generalizations are false, including this one.
  —*Mark Twain*

Since I brought up accounting and financials, let me give you an example of how things can go bad, even when you might think that you have done something good.

This is when you become convinced that you are comparing "apples to apples" when you are really comparing "apples to apple pie," or even something like "Mars to Jupiter."

More importantly, it's when someone is trying to pull a false comparison on you.

In my examples above:

Well, they both *involve* apples right?

Well, they *are* both planets, right?

Answer:

Yes, but no!

The "same" yet radically different!

Obviously.

Let's take a more practical example that might not be so obvious:

Let's say you oversee a manufacturing facility in California that makes some sort of "widget."

Let's say your buddy Pedro oversees a very similar facility in Mexico that makes the exact same widget for the same company you work for.

Your regional VP shows up, slams down a copy of Pedro's labor in front of you and demands to know why your labor cost is "so high" in comparison to Pedro's.

Now, if you are not privy to Pedro's wages or to his financials, you might not know that Pedro is paying his employees only about half of what you are paying yours. You might not know that Pedro actually uses more "man-hours" of labor than you do producing said "widget." What you might not know is that, compared side by side, your facility is actually far *more* efficient.

Here's my point:

When you are comparing things or especially *when someone is trying to do it for you,* make sure that the comparison is valid.

Make sure that you are more or less comparing "apples to friggin' apples" and not "apples" to "pizza" or whatever.

Don't let yourself become the victim of a "false comparison" or "false analogy."

Once again, here is where mastery of the CP comes in.

Things that on the surface might look very similar often are *very* different when you fully examine them.

Note: I wrote a much longer version of a false comparison that you will find in the appendix. I decided it was too boring to include in the main text, but it's brilliant! I call it "Fish Tacos." Check it out later if you need to read something that will put you to sleep.

1.38 Negotiation

I'm not going to spend a bunch of time on this topic. There are plenty of good sources out there that can teach you the basics way better than I can.

My favorite one of all time is Roger Dawson's "Secrets of Power Negotiating."

Anyway, let me just say this about negotiation:

If you want to be a great manager, it is imperative that you hone your negotiating skills.

For example:

You should *know* that when someone says "no" to you in a negotiation, that you should consider it simply to be an "opening position" as opposed to anything close to the "final" word.

You should *know* that when someone says "we've never done that for anyone" or that "we have a strict rule against that," that such a statement doesn't necessarily have anything to do with what *you* are proposing. They had never landed a man on the moon before they did it and "rules" were broken in order to get it done!

You should *know* that when someone says they can't make the decision on something because they are not authorized, they are utilizing a standard negotiation tactic called "appeal to higher authority," and that your next move would be to find out exactly who that higher authority is and get to them.

Here is the most important one:

You should know that unless you have "walk away power" and *the other side does as well,* there is no real negotiation that is going to take place.

For example, let's talk about your salary:

Do you have enough resources to quit your job at any time? If the answer is "no," then when your annual salary review comes up, just realize that you are not really negotiating and that your bosses are really just *telling* you what your raise is or isn't going to be.

Conversely, let's say you're just crazy or you do have the resources and wherewithal to quit your job at any time. Let's say you can actually quit and are prepared to do so if you cannot reach a salary agreement you are happy with.

In that case, and only in that case, *you are negotiating*!

While we're on this topic:

Just for fun, I'm going to give you some of my favorite salary/annual review negotiating ploys/hits of "all time" so you know when *someone is using them on you*:

Jelly-O-Month:

This is when you sit down with your boss and he starts "adding up" all of the money and benefits you *already* have and trying to make the list as long as possible. It's usually accompanied by the phrase "call it."

"Dave, I'd really like to give you a raise, but first let's review *what you already make*. Let's see: your salary of 'call it' X, your free meals 'call it' Y, your expense account 'call it' Z, and so forth…"

In fact, really what your boss is saying is that *you* already "make" so much you should be ashamed for even being in his/her office and you should be very happy that for "this" year—you are getting a yearlong membership in the "Christmas Vacation" Jelly-O-Month Club and that he's not thinking of firing you.

Thank you Clark Griswold!

Ah ha haa! You just got f——d!

Best of Times/Worst of Times:

This is when the bosses explain to you that although your performance was outstanding they can't really give you more than X.

"Sure, the company is doing great, and you were sensational. But what if the economy turns. Everyone knows there is another recession just around the corner, right? We'd hate to come back and have to reduce your salary or bonus. Right?"

Or—and this is the easy one:

"Dave as you know, we didn't make our outlandish projections this year. Oh, you were outstanding. It's just—as I am sure you can see—the economy is not so good and the company is suffering. You don't have a problem suffering as well, do you Dave?"

I'd Like to But:

This is when your boss uses the classic "appeal to higher authority" ploy on you.

"I'd like to give you a bigger raise, Dave, but the ownership just won't go along with it. I mean—you don't want me to actually challenge the ownership on this? Do ya Dave?"

Ah ha haa! You just got f——d! Again!

No One:

This is when you hear this:

"No one ever gets more than X. That's just the way we operate. Call it a 'rule' or whatever, but we just don't give more than X. You understand, right, Dave? Trust me on this, Dave, no one has ever gotten *more* than you are getting."

Or...

"Just so you know, Dave, no one is getting a raise."

Or...

"Just so you know, everybody is getting X percent."

If you believe that, then, what's that story about that bridge for sale?

Performance Picking:

This is when your boss starts off the conversation by listing every single fault he/she can find with your performance.

"Overall, you were great, Dave. But, *this* happened and *this* happened and *this* happened and *this* happened. In fact, now that we think about it, we're wondering why we even said anything nice about you in the first place. In fact, you should be happy to have your job at all. Right, Dave?"

This is a pretty nasty tactic, but some bosses have no problem laying it on you.

Ah ha haa! You just got royally f—d! Again!

And, of course, my all-time favorite kick in the balls…

It's America:

This is when you take a stand, really on anything, but particularly your compensation. At the end of a long conversation of stating your case for a raise, *especially if you made a good one,* your boss will say something like this:

"I know you're disappointed, Dave, but we want you to be happy. This is all we can offer you, Dave, but if you're not satisfied we will completely understand if you leave."

Ugh. The ultimate ball-buster and test of your own "walk-away" power. As I mentioned, if you don't have "walk-away" power, you weren't really negotiating anything in the first place.

Anyway, I encourage you to learn everything you can about negotiating. Become well versed on it so that you can easily spot tactics that are being used on you.

Remember—whenever you hear:

"No."

"Never happens."

"No one ever…"

"It's a rule…"

"We want you to be happy…"

It's BULLSHIT!!!

Note: Now that you know, *please do not use any of the above on someone else*—think of some other way that perhaps involves *the truth*!

Observation: It is interesting to me that so many managers

that have been the regular victims of the *exact* tactics mentioned above throughout their own careers, seem to have no problem using them on their subordinates whenever they have the opportunity. It's as if they've adopted an "I've always gotten F-d, so now you're gonna get F-d" mentality. I don't get it.

1.39 Push Back

This seems like a nice opportunity to talk about push back.

Have you ever had your boss or bosses suggest something that you knew was just about the "dumbest" thing imaginable?

Of course you have!

Me too! Me too! Many more times than I can count.

Incidentally, that's mostly what corporate guys are for!

Warning!

Be very careful how you handle objections to their outlandish proposals, otherwise you might be accused of "pushing back," which is somehow one of the worst "sins" you can commit as a manager.

In fact, it's sort of weird if you think about it. You would imagine that anyone confident enough of mandating an operational change would also be confident enough about said "change" to welcome a challenge to it, particularly from the individual or individuals you were ordering to carry out said change. Particularly since those individuals are probably the real experts!

Not how it works!

They get their feelings hurt—especially if they are Amiables—yikes! Then they get mad. Then they categorize you:

"Oh, that person pushes back on *everything*."

Translation:

"That person is an uncooperative *asshole*."

Not good, especially if it's coming from your "most important customer."

Now, I have to tell you that I'm pretty opinionated about everything—which you might already have determined—and I don't like change, particularly when it involves messing with something that is *already working*!

"If it isn't broken, don't fix it"—right?

Examples:

One time, when I was still a young banquet manager, my GM

actually suggested that rather than change to clean tablecloths after a banquet, I should instead "just flip them" over to their "clean" side.

Ugh.

I mean, how do you even respond to that? Anyway, this guy was so tight and so under pressure to make his "numbers" that he would try almost anything to save a buck.

Now, you're going to ask me:

Is that the same asshole that forced you to push around a gigantic banquet vacuum cleaner that didn't work?

Yes!

Another time, when I was a corporate catering director, the corporate sales guys decided that they wanted to "immediately" roll out a new catering computer program company wide.

Now, at the time, no one in the company besides accounting had even really *seen* a computer—mid 1980s—let alone programmed one!

But, the sales guys were adamant that with "a few written instructions"…

Yeah, right.

I suggested that we might want to go to the properties and at least "train them."

Nope.

The roll out, of course, was a disaster.

Me?

"Dave is an uncooperative asshole."

In fact, I think I was actually *blamed* for it failing!

Anyway, on both of those occasions and countless others, when I strongly objected, I was accused of "pushing back."

Yes, the ultimate sin.

Note: someone referring to you as "pushing back" is basically the same thing as referring to you as "not a team player." Ugh.

Now, let me caution you on the flipside:

I have also "pushed back" on some very good ideas as well. Not only ideas my bosses have proposed, but also on *some from my staff.*

Change is not necessarily a four letter word.

Just most of the time.

This is where the Creative Process comes in.

Before you automatically reject any idea:

Stop

Collaborate—with yourself and/or others.

Action—then open your big mouth.

Result—probably a more intelligent reply than the one you initially thought of.

Measure—maybe you won't be cast as a "pusher back."

Here's the thing:

There are definitely times to push back and times not to.

I've learned to pick my battles.

Sometimes, even if I strongly object to an idea because I know it's goofy, I'll just implement it anyway without comment just to watch the disaster ensue!

Ah ha haa! That's the best!

Sometimes, I surprise myself with the result. Sometimes the goofy idea that *I was sure* would fail actually works! Yikes!

Lastly—and this is important—since I have been wrong about which ideas would work and which wouldn't *so many times* this is what I say to remind me of that fact:

I thought I was right.

I was sure I was right.

I was absolutely positive that I was right.

And... I was wrong!

To know that you know what you know, and that you do not know what you do not know, that is true wisdom.
–Confucius

Anyway, nowadays, if the bosses insist on something I think is goofy, I make a judgment call about whether it's immoral or illegal or if it might kill someone.

If none of the above, I just go ahead and implement it to the best of my ability and wait and secretly hope for it to fail!

Woo hoo!

1.40 Yes, We Can't

Speaking of "push back":

You know that certain famous department store that begins with an N? The one that, no matter what happens there, you end up feeling pretty good when you leave? In fact, even if they don't have anything the size you want or the style you want or whatever, you still "feel" pretty good when you finally walk out.

Why?

Because someone has done a masterful job of creating a culture that has taken "no" out of their staff's vocabulary.

I like to put my own twist on the elimination of "no":

"Yes!"—*we can't!*

"Absolutely"—*not!*

"Very possibly"—*never going to happen.*

"Let me check on that"—*also, never going to happen.*

Example:

Let's say you've just arrived at your hotel after a long trip and you are exhausted. Let's say it's only about 11am, so you nicely ask the desk clerk if it's possible to check in early.

Now, let's say that said desk clerk knows that the hotel was full the night prior and there is no way an early check in is going to happen.

The clerk has two options for an answer to your question.

He can say:

"No, sir. The hotel is very busy."

Or he could say:

"Yes, sir. One moment, sir. Let me check on that for you."

PS—if the clerk is really good, he/she will get *your name* in there.

Now, you observe the clerk checking his computer and/or going to the back office or whatever. He or she is definitely looking… looking…

Finally, after a lot of gyrations and obvious effort, the clerk turns to you and says:

"I'm so sorry Mr./Mrs./Miss So-and-so, I have tried *everything*, but I think 4pm is about the best I can do."

Both answers were essentially "no," right?

Which one was better?

Obviously, the second.

Remember when we talked about "perception?"

Want to be "perceived" as a much more positive person without essentially changing anything about what you actually "do" about anything?

Suggestion:

Remove "no" from your vocabulary.

Then, the proper "first" reaction to a question regardless of what the "ultimate" answer is going to be is:

"Yes, let me see!"

Or…

"Let me think about that."

Or …

"Possibly."

Or…

Anyway, I'm still working on it.

1.41 The Power of "No"

Speaking of "no"…

This is sort of chapter B to "Yes, we can't."

Confession time again:

I love the word "no."

As I mentioned, I'm an English Lit major, so "words" are kind of my "thing."

For example:

I also love the words "moist" and "cheese" and "meat," but mostly just because I like the way they sound when spoken.

Try saying "meat," and then, try saying, "meet."

Totally different, right?

Meat! Love *that* word!

I love the word "no" for another reason. Not for the way it sounds as much as what it allows me *not to do*!

In fact, "no" often means:

I DON'T HAVE TO DO ANYTHING!

It's the laziest word in the English Language—and in any other translation in any other language for that matter.

Think about it:

Get a job?

No. Rather be poor.

Take wife to movies?

No. Rather sit on my ass in front of TV.

Wash car?

No. Rather leave it dirty. It's just going to get dirty again.

Wipe ass?

See "wash car" above.

Do something "nice" for someone other than myself?

Ah ha haaaaaa!!

See what I mean? If I say "yes" to any of the above and/or the list of 1,000 other things we could quickly think of, it means:

I might *have to do something*!

Anyway, I don't know how your mind works, but mine has a "default mode" that is programmed to initially respond "no" to almost anything.

This is not good.

"Would you like to…"

"No."

"How about…?"

"No."

Incidentally, my brilliant wife has figured this out about me, so she no longer puts things as a request or question:

"I bought tickets to the movies."

"Oh, okay."

"Get in the bedroom…"

"Oh, okay."

Remember when we had the conversation about the Creative Process?

Bingo!

Before you say "no" you need to *stop and think about it.*

Now, there are some things that *actually do* require a "no" answer.

And, just as I have become an expert at giving "no" as an answer, some people can't seem to say the word at all *when they need to*:

"Can I borrow your car?"

"Are you coming over for Christmas?"

"Would you like to go to dinner with…?"

"Can we get a cat?"

"You don't mind if I...?"

No, you cannot borrow my car because the last time you did you brought it back dirty with the gas on E. In fact, you always bring it back that way.

No, I am not going to come over for Christmas, because the family fights the whole time, someone gets drunk, and I am miserable being there the whole time I'm there.

No, we are not going to dinner because the last four times I picked up the check and I was miserable the whole time thinking about what a cheap...

No, we are definitely not getting a cat!

Yes, in fact, I *do* mind! You didn't *thank me* the last time!

The word "no" is a great word to have in your arsenal and you might need it:

Once again, pause before you use it, but don't be afraid to use it as your "final" answer when necessary.

1.42 Parachutes

Definition of insanity:

Doing the same thing over and over again and expecting a different or better result.

Ugh!

Sorry.

I know it's an old and worn out phrase, but it really applies in management, especially when you keep doing things and getting a "bad" result over and over *and yet you keep doing it*!

Sometimes what I call "parachutes" are the answer.

Example:

Let's say you have an area of your department that absolutely will not function correctly without at least 5 staff members to do whatever the job is. Unfortunately for you, almost every day or at least a few times a week, one of those "critical" staff members has some sort of problem and doesn't show up.

Now, you can either keep scheduling 5 people a day and continue to have that area unravel several times a week...

Or...

You can schedule 6.

That way, if one of them doesn't show you are still going to be able to function.

Now, your bosses might say you can't do that. They might say you cannot afford the additional labor.

Fine.

Then be prepared to have that area constantly screwed up.

Or...

Figure out how it can run efficiently with only 4 staffers.

Or...

Cross-train someone or a few someone/s who can be pulled over from a less critical area.

Or...

Fire the person/s in that area that constantly no-show and hire some replacements that like to show up for work.

Here's my point:

If some area in your management sphere—or in your life for that matter—is not working, *you need to change it*!

Sometimes the change might make things worse. If so, change them again until you get it right.

Here's another example I may have mentioned earlier:

When I was first in catering, we had this bad problem of banquet event orders going "missing."

This was back in the days of the typewritten 4-part form—yes, with an actual typewriter—where the catering coordinator would type it then distribute as follows:

1 to the customer

1 to the chef

1 to the banquet department

And 1 that stayed in the catering office in a 3 ring binder we called the "bible."

Now, most of the time, that system worked. But often, we might have 30-60 events per day, and inevitably one of those forms wouldn't make it to someone; the chef, or banquets, or both!

First "parachute":

I had the coordinators check the "bible" against what the chef had and banquets had for the following day.

Result:

Worked most of the time, but somewhere between the "day prior" and the "day of" someone still managed to sometimes "lose" a banquet event order.

Chaos!

The chef didn't cook the food or the banquet department hadn't set the room or…

Second "parachute":

I had the PM captain check the "bible" against what the banquet department and the chef had for the next day *again* at or near the end of his/her shift.

Result:

We hardly ever missed a banquet event order. But, we still missed one once in a rare while.

Third "parachute":

I had the morning captain or banquet manager run through all of the banquet event orders *again* with the chef and banquets first thing that day.

Result:

I don't recall ever "missing" a banquet event order again.

Here's the point:

Check…

Check…

And triple check…

Or…

Change and/or modify something that isn't "working" until it does—and it does consistently:

If you're still having trouble or maybe when you *first* have trouble, remember:

"It's already been done."

Someone has already perfected whatever you are trying to fix.

1.43 Tools

Give your staff the proper tools.

I know that seems like a no-brainer that is hardly worth mentioning, but I have run across this issue so many times in my career that I just have to say something.

You might recall my story about the GM I once worked for that was too cheap to buy my banquet department a new vacuum.

Stupid.

I remember watching a documentary about World War II and the US submarine commanders insisting that the torpedoes they were using didn't detonate when they hit their targets! Apparently, no one up the chain of command believed them *because none of the brass up the chain of command ever got on a sub*!

How about not ever having enough silverware to set up with?

How about having to go search for enough linen to make up rooms?

How about someone forced to work with a crappy computer when working on a computer is what he or she is primarily paid to do?

Stupid.

Here is where the old saying "pound wise and penny foolish" comes in.

Give your staff the proper tools to do their job.

You'll know if you *ask them.*

You'll find out for sure by MBWA!

Get on the "sub!"

If you have to fight the bosses for enough money to get those tools—do so!

This is where having good negotiating skills will come in.

Also, be prepared to ask as many times as it takes.

News flash:

It might take 10 requests. It might take 20!

It shouldn't, but sometimes it does. Do it!

Know the facts. Be prepared to make your case.

I especially like this one:

"Aren't we *paying* them to ...?"

1.44 Lobster

This chapter pertains to not getting lost in the minutia.

Example:

When I worked for a hotel company that focused a lot of attention on the food and beverage operations, we always had lots of help from the "corporate" guys about saving money.

I often found myself sitting in long meetings—well, they weren't meetings because they always went on and on for way more than an hour—where we would discuss things like saving a few cents on a number 10 can of tomato paste by purchasing such-and-such brand from such-and-such company at such-and-such-volumes.

That would have been brilliant except for one thing:

While all of the managers were "in a meeting" beating their heads on the conference table over the price of tomato paste, lobsters were disappearing out the back door of the hotel!

We would have known that if we had been paying attention

to the big holes in the operation instead of having our heads up our butts trying to count "paperclips."

If, instead of trying to save money on the purchase of silverware, we had been paying attention to how much additional labor we were using trying to run down what little we had in the hotels.

If...

If...

Here's my point:

Before you let some Analytical convince you to focus your attention on a half-hour of labor, or the counting of paperclips, or whatever, look for the "lobster" *first*.

And, there is always a "lobster" somewhere. Sometimes there are a bunch of them practically swimming right out your back door.

Now, when you have honed your operation to such a "razor's edge" that you have completely exhausted the hunt for any "big" opportunities—then fine, *you're amazing*—start counting the number of copies someone is running on the copier!

1.45 Sops

Standard Operating Procedures

Ugh!

Okay, you may have to have them—especially if you have a bunch of Analyticals working for you or you happen to work for a bunch of them.

But…

In general…

Big thick SOP manuals are useless.

In your business, ask yourself this:

When was the last time anyone referred to one?

If the answer is *frequently*, then you probably need a SOP manual.

If the answer is *rarely*, if ever, then you probably don't even need one.

Note: Most corporate guys love SOP manuals.

Why?

They are usually the guys who were paid way too much to write them.

I know. I was once one of them.

Anyway:

If I were ever going to write my "dream" SOP manual for hospitality it would only be four words long:

Use your common sense.

Well… five words. But I don't want to be admonished.

1.46 Kiss

Yes:

Keep it simple stupid.

We're back to that again!

I know this seems obvious, but I'm only bringing it up again because *so many managers violate this important rule.*

As managers, *our job is to figure out how to make things simpler for our staff,* not more difficult or harder.

Note: Corporate guys—I'm particularly speaking to you!

Now, sometimes, in order to improve your product, you may "need to" implement some procedures that "make things harder" for your staff.

That's fine, provided you do the following:

Make sure you actually "need to" *before* you implement said procedures.

If you have the opportunity to "test" the new procedure before rolling it out—*do so*!

Make sure you have fully explained, trained, and tooled your staff regarding said procedures.

Make sure it's something you'd be willing to do yourself.

When you "add" a task to someone's job description, try to "remove" another at the same time—*maybe two or three.*

Look as hard for the opportunities to "simplify" as you do to "complicate."

Make sure you "monitor" the progress MBWA and admit defeat *early* if the new procedures don't work out the way you initially dreamed.

Here's the point:

In my business, the more I can simplify things for my staff, the less opportunity for mistakes, confusion and needless frustration.

1.47 Office Politics and Back Stabbing

It's not "he doesn't have to shoot you now," it's "he doesn't have to shoot me now!"

—*Daffy Duck*

Remember when our mommy used to tell us:

"If you can't say something nice about someone, don't say anything at all."

Yeah, right.

We promptly ignored her and started spreading shit around about anybody and everybody.

Guilty!

Don't do it!

Oh, you are going to be tempted.

Especially as a mid-manager, there is going to be a time when you are in the office with your boss (or bosses) and they are going to be maligning one of your co-managers or co-workers and you are just going to eat it up.

You, falsely, are going to think that because your bosses are being so open with you about your co-worker's incompetence *that you are not in the same club*!

Especially if you view the co-worker in question as some sort of "rival," you are just going to love the fact that your bosses think that he/she is a POS.

Now, never mind the fact that your bosses are making a huge management mistake by carrying on like that, I'm pretty sure that is not going to occur to you. It should.

Here's what really happens:

The minute *you* are out of the office, your bosses will likely switch topics.

Instead of maligning your co-worker, they will almost certainly be maligning *you*!

I could tell you a hundred stories of these types of experiences over the course of my career.

Sadly, I have to admit some participation.

Here's my point:

As a boss yourself, don't let yourself be tempted—when one of your staff or managers is in the room—to malign another of their co-workers.

As a manager—don't let yourself be tempted to join in the fray when one of your direct associates is under fire.

As I said, I've done it.

It's fun!

Guilty!

Nothing good can come of it.

Remember:

When *you* are in the room, you're great and your co-worker is shit.

When you are *not* in the room, your co-worker may or may not be shit, but *you* most certainly are!

Let the bosses rant.

Stay out of it.

1.48 Effective Immediately

Effective immediately—the beatings will continue until morale improves!

Those two words put together in any memo or announcement annoy me so much I'm going to give them their own short chapter.

This is my opinion about "effective immediately" notifications:

It means someone managerially F-D up!

Big time!

Whoever issued them discovered something, or realized something that they *should have already known* about, but *didn't* for whatever reason.

Or, they think that a new policy is *so important* that they need to emphasize it by tagging it "effective immediately."

Effective immediately—stop drinking the bottled water! For guest use only!

Effective immediately—stop harassing the ducks in the pond.

Effective immediately—lunches are to be taken between 1PM and 2PM only!

Effective immediately—there will be no more employee parking in the lower lot.

Here is my advice:

Go ahead.

When you discover that the ducks are being harassed, *change the policy.*

But, just because *you weren't paying attention* and didn't know about the "ducks," don't "panic" and throw out some goofy announcement with the EI header.

Why?

Because it tells your entire staff just that!

That is:

That you weren't paying attention, and when you finally found out about "whatever," you just about "shit" yourself.

That may be true.

You may have missed something or made a mistake.

No reason to announce it.

On the other hand:

If you want to announce the fact that *you* missed something *you* shouldn't have and *scream it to the world*, just write this on your memo header:

EFFECTIVE IMMEDIATELY

The Amiables on your staff—and remember, *they are all Amiables*—will hate you.

1.49 It's Already Been Done

You know those easily stacking food cans?

I invented those.

In fact, I've invented a whole bunch of really cool products over the years only to find out that *someone else beat me to the punch.* Not only had they already invented those products, their version was almost always *better than mine.*

Ask me if I hate Air BNB!

Done!

Tracking device for your dog?

Done!

Personalized emoji app?

Done!

Also done:

Man on the moon?

Yep!

How to negotiate?

Books and books on the subject.

Management?

Well… obviously.

Here's my point:

Before you shit yourself over what seems to be a new problem or you try to build a better mousetrap—research it!

If you find yourself struggling with virtually *anything*, remember that someone else has already figured out how to do it or fix it.

1.50 When in Doubt—Hire A Professional

Speaking of "already been done":

This is chapter B to it.

One time my washing machine suddenly started leaking water. There was some sort of problem with my discharge line so I decided—drum roll—*to try to fix it myself.*

Missssstake! I don't know anything about fixing a washing machine.

Anyway, after about an hour, several bloody knuckles and a bunch of miscellaneous screws in an old coffee cup, I decided to surrender and call in an expert.

Darren the Appliance Doctor showed up a couple of hours later. In ten minutes, he had the entire washer disassembled. Ten minutes after that, he had replaced the broken part, re-assembled the washer, and it was purring like a kitten with no sign of leaking.

Let me give you another example that is less obvious but one of my career favorites:

One time, when I was working in a corporate office, someone decided that we should change up the room amenities. You know, the little hotel soaps, shampoos and lotions that we all love so much?

Okay, fine.

Good idea.

Let's upgrade!

Suddenly, I found myself in a room of all males "testing"—drum roll—*lotion*!

We were rubbing it on our hands and sniffing it like we really knew something.

It was—uh—one of the most ridiculous situations I have ever had the pleasure of being a part of. Six or seven grown men smearing lotion all over the place!

Ah ha haaa!

Not to be sexist, but maybe we should have asked some women? Maybe survey some hotel customers in general?

All I know for sure is this: *we were not qualified.*

If we were... well... I'm not even going to get into that.

Here's my point once again:

Whatever you are struggling to do, or trying to do, there is someone out there in the world who already knows how to do it or is way more qualified to make the decision!

Planning a redesign?

Hire a designer.

Plumbing problem?

Licensed plumber please.

Brain surgery?

Well-referenced neurosurgeon.

Lotion selection?

Ah ha haa!

1.51 Hiring Staff

I'm not going to bore you with a bunch of "criteria" that will supposedly make you great at hiring great staff members.

Once again, there are plenty of resources out there you can research on your own that will supposedly give you the "clues."

Having said that:

I still think hiring good people is mostly "gut instinct" if you want to know the truth.

Of course, appearance, first impressions, resume, references, all play a part in any hiring decision.

Sometimes you get "lucky" and hire a "superstar." But, they're rare.

This is sort of my interview formula:

I like to give prospective staff the "dark side" as well as the "bright side" of working for me so I don't have to apologize later.

Whenever possible, I like to hire seemingly "over-qualified" individuals provided I've grilled them to my satisfaction on "why" they might want to take a lesser job.

I like to *make sure* prospects fully understand the *exact* pay and benefit package. I've found in too many instances that they are too afraid to ask and quit later when they find out what the "real deal" is.

I sometimes hire and/or have my managers hire prospects we "know" or "think" are "superstars" even if we don't "really have a spot for them at the moment." We will.

Anyway, my personal experience with hiring "superstars" is about one in ten—and I think I'm pretty good at hiring.

"Superstars" are rare.

Here's how you'll figure out if you're good:

You will end up turning the other "nine" into "superstars!"

If you can do that, you'll know you're a damn good manager.

1.52 Money Doesn't Just Talk

It screams!

And, it can scream both ways—good and bad.

This is where the old saying "underpromise and overdeliver" really comes into play.

Here are the two basic rules I like to use regarding my staff and money:

Never promise anything you are not 100% positive you can deliver.

Once given, you can *never* take it away and it can *never* be "less" than it was.

Example:

Once I was "promised" a catering director promotion to a new hotel in the company that was just being built, which would have resulted in a significant raise in pay. Unfortunately, as it turned out, my "boss" didn't actually have the "final" say in the hiring decision and the GM of the hotel had other ideas about whom he wanted in the position.

My boss had made a mistake. He was not actually the final decision maker, so he shouldn't have promised me the promotion.

One time, as a catering director, I had my bonus reduced because my department was doing "so well" the bosses decided that my bonus formula—which was tied to revenue—was too high and that I was making too much money, so they arbitrarily reduced it.

I could go on.

Anyway:

Operating in such a manner—I would propose—is not a good way to win over your staff.

Rather:

Don't make promises you are not sure you can keep.

Don't tell someone you are going to promote them until you have the "official" memo in your hand.

Don't announce a raise or the money involved until you have the "official" memo in your hand.

Regarding bonus money:

I know the Analyticals prefer that bonuses be tied to performance and you may be in a business where this is the norm and it simply cannot be avoided. In that case, make sure someone does the math in advance so that you *never* have to go back to that staffer and tell him or her that they've "overperformed" and you'll have to reduce it!

Ugh!

At this point, I think that bonuses, where possible, should be tied to "nothing" besides your own arbitrary judgment—keeping in mind, of course, the rule that they must *never* be less than they were before.

What about in times of severe financial crisis? What if the company is experiencing a particularly tough time? Can salaries and bonuses be reduced then?

Maybe, with a lot of apologizing you might get away with pay or benefit reduction.

But—and this is the big BUT—you better not get amnesia when times improve and "forget" to increase said pay, benefits, or bonuses to former levels or greater when the company has recovered.

You might not remember the reductions, but anyone working for you surely will.

Lastly, remember this:

It's never enough.

Regarding what you pay or bonus your staff:

It's never enough.

The only thing worse:

Reducing what you have already given them.

1.53 It's All About The Money

Remember when I said that, as a manager, it's not about the money?

Well, that only applies to *you* and *your* salary.

As far as your company is concerned regarding revenue and costs, it's nothing but *all about the money*!

In fact, money screams far more loudly up the corporate ladder than down it.

Here's how:

Nothing will endear you more to the corporation or ownership group or boss that you work for than *making them money*!

Conversely, nothing will alienate them more quickly than if you don't.

Maybe it has something to do with the fact that making money is the primary reason that they've invested in the business. I mean, everyone knows that one of the main definitions of a "corporation" centers on making money for its shareholders.

Go figure.

Anyway, similar to coaches in professional sports, who are generally considered only as good as their last few games, managers are generally only as good as their last few financial statements.

In sports, great coaches are the ones who have figured out how to win. In management, great managers are generally the ones who have figured out how to *make money*—lots of it.

In some cases, managers who are not directly involved in revenue production might just be great because they excel in cost controls. Same difference.

"I'm too busy with day to day operational issues to figure out ways to make more money," you say.

Then you are not effectively delegating.

"I've looked at everything in my department from one end to the other, and there is simply no way to increase revenue or cut costs."

No, you haven't. There is a "lobster" hiding somewhere. Find it.

"Really, I've looked for the 'lobster' and there simply isn't one."

Invent one. You are not using the Creative Process effectively.

Here's my point, and I can only speak from my own personal experience:

In my life, I have never taken over a paper route, a kitchen, a hotel department, a hotel, or even a series of hotels, where there wasn't some major opportunity or even a bunch of them left "on the table" from previous management.

Further, to my great astonishment and chagrin, for as "great" as I may claim to be, I have also been in the embarrassing position of having managers follow me who have found opportunities later that even I didn't see.

Anyway, here are just some of the obvious advantages of making more money than "the other guy":

Generally, you can operate your department or business the way you want to with way less interference from your boss or ownership.

You can more easily convince ownership to give you the tools and/or staffing that you desire.

You can more easily convince the ownership to give your staff the money and/or rewards you would like to give them for *helping* you make the ownership more money.

You will have a way less difficult time getting the 3-5% annual raise I promised you earlier!

You can stay employed!

Here's the big one:

You can have the personal satisfaction of knowing that—given all of the above—you are making your bosses and/or ownership group more than almost any other manager could make them!

1.54 Thank Yous

You cannot thank people enough.

Did I say you cannot thank people enough?

I meant, *you CANNOT thank people enough*!

Have you ever been thanked enough?

I didn't think so.

Now, as I mentioned earlier, I'm a Driver type concerned mostly with myself, so it is not a natural thing for me to give a shit about anyone else, particularly my staff. I walk around in a world that is primarily *all about me*.

And, after all, aren't "they" getting paid to do whatever they are doing?

Do I have to thank them *too*?

Ugh!

On the other hand, another big part of my personality is Amiable. So how do you think I "feel" when people, bosses or whoever *don't thank me?*

Yikes!

Anyway, I literally had to "train" myself to thank people. My mother, in her defense, did her best to instill a sense of this in me at an early age, so perhaps "re-train" would be fairer to her.

Here's my point:

Even if you already "think" you are pretty good at thanking people, look again!

Do you walk around your department thanking people for the "normal" job they are doing for you?

Do you have meetings where you call out not only certain individuals, but also your entire staff?

Do you write *handwritten* notes of thanks?

Do you actually tip instead of "just thinking about it?"

Have you ever thanked your garbage man?

Have you ever tipped your garbage man?

Here's my even bigger point:

"Thinking" about thanking someone is *not* thanking them.

"Thinking" about handwriting a note and mailing it to someone who did something nice for you is *not* the same thing as doing it!

"Thinking" about tipping your housekeeper in a hotel is *not* the same thing as doing it!

By now you might have surmised that I think that money needs to be somehow involved with all forms of thanks.

Not always.

With your family or people that you know?

Certainly not. That's why they invented hand-written notes and phone calls.

With your staff or people who have performed a service for you?

Not always, but some of the time.

It mostly depends on whether or not you are trying to say thank you in all caps!

Money doesn't just say "thank you," it says "THANK YOU!"

Here's what I have found:

In business, I have been fortunate enough to work for some bosses who largely subscribe a philosophy of being generous to their staff as a smart business move, so I have been able to be very generous to my staff above and beyond their "normal" compensation.

In my personal life, being overly "tight" in the interest of fiscal responsibility is really only an excuse to be overly "tight." I'd rather be poor.

In fact, I am poor, but I spread a lot of money around to people who have been of service to me.

Try this:

Every once in a while, go out in front of your house early in the morning, maybe around the holidays, and hand the garbage guys some money along with a big verbal "thank you" for hauling your shit away all year.

When you see their reaction, it just might become a tradition!

Also, if and when we go out to lunch or dinner, we are *not* splitting the check, okay?

Either *you* are picking it up or *I am going to*!

My god!

Here's the most important point about "thank yous"—money or no:

Don't bother thanking anyone for anything if you *don't believe it*!

There's nothing worse than getting "thanked" by someone who is *not sincere.*

Nothing!

Nothing!

1.55 Perspective

Speaking of picking up the restaurant check:

Do you think you are going to live forever?

I know a bunch of people who act like they are going to live forever.

My experience teaches me that this is simply not the case. In fact, I've lost so many relatives, friends and other people that I have known to premature causes of death, that it seems like an early and unexpected departure from this earth is much more likely than a long and protracted one.

Sometimes, I feel like I am the only one aware of this fact.

When you croak, you know what you get for all of that anxiety and stress you had regarding that last financial statement or the fact that Billy wrecked the van or someone missed their flight because they didn't get their wake-up call on time?

As I mentioned before:

A short email from your boss to the entire management team about what a well liked and integral part of the corporation you were and how you will be missed and also—to please forward all of *your* emails to *so-and-so* until they find your replacement which will be shortly!

That's it!

Did I say that's it?

I meant—*that's it*!

The only reason I'm bringing this up is because I think sometimes putting one's own relatively "insignificant existence" into perspective once in a while is good for the calming of the nerves.

In fact, there's not really much to get upset about, if you really think about it.

Didn't kill anyone today?

Good.

Relax.

Your time is coming.

Enjoy the fact that you are still "here" as long as you are still "here."

Having "problems" means you are still alive.

Take your vacation.

Go for that walk.

Take that class.

Do something nice for yourself or someone else.

And…

For God's sake, get off your cheap ass and go out and *tip the garbage guy*!

Lastly:

If you ever try to split a dinner check again with *anyone*—I'm gonna scream!

1.56 Trouble

I want to briefly discuss this again just because "trouble" seems to present itself so often managerially and in life.

We need to be ready.

In the late eighties, there was a cop show that some of you who are old enough might remember, called Miami Vice.

The main character was a "super cool" vice cop named Sonny Crockett, well played by Don Johnson. Sonny was a good looking, mid-thirties, super "with it" cop that drove a Ferrari and lived on his own sailboat with a pet alligator!

What could be cooler than *that*?

Well, I wanted to *be* Sonny Crockett! I was in my early twenties at the time and I really wanted to be Sonny—or at least be as cool as he was.

Anyway, in one episode, he and his new partner Rico Tubbs were staked out at a hotel pool. It was a very hot day, and

Tubbs, fresh in from New York, wasn't used to the extreme Florida heat and was complaining about it.

That's when the magic happened:

Sonny took a long drag off his Marlboro, gazed out at the pool from behind his super-cool Ray-Bans, blew out the smoke and uttered these profound words:

"You just gotta learn to go with the heat, Rico. It's just like life. You just gotta keep telling yourself, no matter how hot it gets, sooner or later, there's going to be a cool breeze blowin' in."

That, my friends, is my favorite quote of all time.

Perfect metaphor for life?

Goofy?

Maybe.

But I'll tell you this—that quote or some shortened version of it has sustained me through some pretty dark and difficult times.

Now, I'm not saying that you are not ever going to experience situations in life that are not going to be justifiably traumatic and upsetting.

Loss of a loved one.

Loss of a job.

Financial trouble.

Death of your favorite pet.

Divorce.

Serious health issues.

The sudden realization that you've raised an asshole.

Anyway, the potential list is long.

I guess if almost anyone wants to think about it long enough, they could all come up with reasons they could and should feel terrible about something.

Hell, sometimes I even feel like shit for *no reason* whatsoever.

Really.

Sometimes I just get up in the morning and feel sad or like shit. No reason.

It happens.

More often, I blow a "small" problem up into a "big" one.

It's not my fault.

I came off the assembly line that way.

"Baditude."

My solution to these psychological "emergencies" however "big" or "small" is to attempt to put my own personal situation into perspective:

I think about the inevitable email that's coming. You know, the one that is going to announce my death and to please forward…

I sometimes go to the beach and pick up a handful of sand and try to find the one small grain of it that represents all of my troubles as they pertain to the universe in general.

I think about something "happy" from the past, present, or that may happen in the future.

I think about the people I love.

I think about how much *I love being alive*—regardless of my shitty and very momentary circumstance.

I think of the "half-full" part of my "glass."

Mostly, I think about how much I now do believe, that if I'm patient, a cool breeze really is going to be blowin' in!

Relax.

You'll be a way better manager and probably lower your blood pressure at the same time.

1.57 No Try

No! Try not! Do or do not. There is no "try." –Yoda Empire Strikes Back.

Another one of my favorite quotes of all time so I have to get this in.

Since we've been talking so much—or at least I have—about the things we *must* do and the things we *must not* in order to be great managers, I just wanted to mention this concept of "try."

In short, using that term is dangerous!

Here's why:

If I ever tell you I am going to "try" to do anything, *it is probably never going to happen.*

"I'll *try* to get you a raise."

Don't say it!

"I'll *try* to get that report to you by Friday."

Nope.

"I'm going to *try* to stop smoking."

Never going to happen.

"I'm going to *try* to write a book."

Ah ha haa!

Try to eliminate "try" from your vocabulary.

Wait!

Let me rephrase that:

Focus on *eliminating* "try" from your vocabulary.

You will get a lot more done—or not.

But…

At least you won't be fooling yourself or others about whether or not "it" is ever going to happen.

Also:

For the very same reasons, beware of the person who tells you they will "try" to do something.

The difference between someone who tells you they "*are* going to do something" as opposed to someone who tells you they are going to "*try* to do something"…

Well…

1.58 Prepare To Fail

Or…

No good deed goes unpunished.

I'm only bringing this up in order to save you from yourself *as a manager.*

You need to know this:

Whatever you do for your staff; the raises you fight for, the bonuses you give them, the schedules you create to benefit their needs instead of the needs of the business, even the amount of times you personally thank them…

It's *never* enough. *It will never be enough*!

The more you give them, the more they will expect.

Period.

The same goes for your bosses and/or the company your work for.

Also:

That "favor" you did for one of your staffers?

Get ready…

Someone else is going to have a problem with it.

Someone is going to attempt to make a big deal out of nothing.

And *you* thought you were just trying to be nice!

I'm not saying this to be negative.

I don't say this to discourage you.

It's just a law of human nature.

Normal.

I say it to remind you that—just when you think you've done something amazing for your staff—it won't be "enough."

Do it anyway.

They might not know you're killing yourself for them, but *you* will.

Your bosses?

Ugh, forget about it.

If it helps, take some consolation in this:

If you are really as good as you think you are—they will all know when you're gone!

1.59 Rating Your Department and/or Yourself

I don't know about you, but over the course of my career my bosses have sometimes been, shall we say "sketchy" regarding feedback.

Some have been critical of my job performance when I felt it had been "stellar." Some of my bosses simply didn't say what they thought.

On occasion—of course, never often enough in my opinion—they would tell me when I did something "right."

After many years, this is what I think about all that:

It is not your boss's responsibility to tell you how you are doing.

It's yours.

Now, you might say:

"Didn't you tell me earlier on that—at work—the "boss" is my most important customer? How am I supposed to know how I'm doing if he/she doesn't tell me?"

Your bosses may not actually "know" how you are doing or they might indeed be "bad" managers with respect to constructive feedback.

Or...

Maybe they do know and just like to see you sweat.

Or...

Maybe you've been criticized when you felt it was unwarranted and you want to "know" for yourself how you're "really" doing.

Or...

Maybe *you* have a problem in your department and you want to figure out what it is yourself.

The answer is simple:

Rate yourself and/or your department.

Okay, this is admittedly a pretty simple idea and it should be obvious. The only reason I bring it up is that it took me a while to figure it out.

Now, of course, "everyone" is rating practically "everything." It's gotten to the point where you get a text three minutes after you leave the grocery store asking how the cashier was.

Use the same tactic on yourself.

Rating yourself or your department works like this:

Let's say you have a department with 5 staff members working for you. Simply rate them on their individual performance from 1-5—with:

1 = F

2 = D

3 = C

4 = B

5 = A

So,

Mark   3

Joe   4

Shelly   5

Anne   2

Don   4

18 total divided by 5 staff = 3.6 or C+

Ugh!

I bet your department, especially as far as you are concerned, runs like a high C.

Here's the point:

Now, if you want to improve your department, you know what to do, right?

Mark and Anne are your immediate "ball and chain."

Here are your choices:

Figure out how to bring up Mark and Anne's performance.

Fire them and replace them with someone who will perform better.

Leave things as they are and continue to function as they are—yikes! C+

By the way, this rating method will work if you oversee several departments or even several hundred employees.

Example:

Maybe the 5 individuals above are all department heads or just the department itself.

As mentioned—and perhaps most importantly—you can also use this method to rate yourself and your own performance.

For example, when I'm running a hotel, I like to ask myself:

How is the hotel doing financially, especially compared to the market?

What is the condition of the hotel given the resources I have to maintain it?

How is the staff overall? Happy? Service oriented? Trained?

How is the hotel perceived in the market?

How is the hotel perceived in the community?

What is the hotel's safety record?

Etc.

If I give the above the 1-5 treatment, and am honest about it, I'll know exactly how I'm doing.

No one will need to tell me.

1.60 The Truth

Now why would I even bring this up again?

Truth?

It seems like a given, right?

Didn't we already discuss this?

Tell the truth?

Simple, right?

Just tell the truth *all the time every time*, right?

Well, telling the truth must be a lot harder than it seems, because my experience with most people is that they tend to lie—and they tend to do it a lot.

Hell, there have been plenty of times in life when that person was *me*!

Guilty!

In fact, especially when I was a kid, I lied a lot. I lied to my mother all the time. I lied to my teachers. I lied to my friends. And, oh yeah—boy did I lie to my girlfriends! Yikes!

Why?

Usually because I'd done something I knew was "wrong" or that I was ashamed of or that I knew was going to disappoint someone. Sometimes it was simply to get something I really wanted.

My mom—in her defense—had made a valiant attempt to teach me early on that lying, stealing and cheating were not necessarily admirable traits. In retrospect, I now realize how much influence she really had in that department. She wasn't able to stop me from doing it, but boy was she effective at making me feel bad about doing it.

Incidentally, did you know that it is virtually impossible to lie if you have no sense of the difference between "right" and "wrong"?

For example:

If you don't think stealing is "wrong" then why would you ever lie about it?

If you had stolen something, you'd just admit it, right?

I suppose you could be an asshole and say that even if you

didn't think stealing was wrong, you might lie about it just to avoid punishment.

Point taken.

But, you're an *asshole.*

Anyway, I blame most of my early lying on simply being an immature asshole.

But, I also blame it on having acquired—very early on in my life—a strong sense of "right" and "wrong." Thanks mom!

I needed to lie because I kept doing stuff that was wrong and I knew that it was wrong.

How did I know it was wrong?

Because it made my gut hurt.

That's how I recognize that something is "wrong"—for me.

Finally, after a number of years, I had what you might call an epiphany!

Ready?

If you stop doing shit that you're ashamed of it is much easier to tell the truth!

If you don't steal stuff...

If you don't cheat...

If you don't basically try to orchestrate the world to work solely in your favor regardless of the consequences to others...

If you don't take the easy way out by lying to someone just in order to spare their feelings or for some other cheesy reason like your own personal gain...

If you quit doing things that make your gut hurt.

If...

If...

If...

Of course, this presupposes that somewhere deep in your moral wheelhouse you actually view such behavior as less than admirable.

It also presupposes that deep down somewhere inside your own soul you actually do value the truth.

It took me a while, but I eventually found out that living as close to my own "core" values as I can just makes life easier. In fact, it took me a while to really grasp that the "truth" was one of them.

Also, I began to realize that most of my "heroes" were people who generally didn't lie.

Remember the *"be a person worth imitating"* thing?

Anyway, over the years I've endeavored to master the *"not lying thing."*

Telling the truth just makes life *easier*.

Now, I'm still not perfect—but I can tell you this:

When it comes down to "brass tacks," I generally tell the truth.

Sometimes it's very hard to do.

Sometimes it's downright painful.

I can also tell you this:

As hard as it may be or as painful, I have found that telling the truth almost always ends up being the best course of action.

And, if I can't tell the truth, then I—usually—opt for the next best thing:

I don't say anything.

For example:

Maybe telling the truth will unnecessarily hurt someone. In that case, I keep my mouth shut.

"Do these pants make me look fat?"

On the other hand:

Sometimes people need to be told the truth, even when you know it is going to hurt them.

Sometimes people need to be told the truth, *just so you can live with yourself.*

Sometimes people need to be told the truth because they are assholes or bullies and someone needs to call them on it.

Sometimes—whatever "it" is—it's just "that" important.

I call that kind of truth telling:

Rectal candor!

Obviously, it is a form of truth telling that should be used sparingly.

In fact, "rectal candor" is the "atom bomb" of truth telling.

Have it in your arsenal, but use it *only* in the event of emergency!

Most people who know me—and *especially* those who know me well—will tell you that I am a "straight shooter."

In other words, that I generally tell the truth.

Really, it's easy. I simply avoid doing anything that I would be so ashamed of that I would have to lie about it if confronted.

If you want to make your life easier, try it for a while and see if I'm right.

Okay...

I'm just about done lecturing you on the virtue of telling the truth. But, I just want to underline one more fact:

It's taken me a lot of years of being a pretty consistent truth teller to gain the reputation of being one.

This matters.

Why?

Because someday when you need it most, you are going to

have to tell someone something that they might not otherwise believe if *it weren't coming from you.*

You will have a literal "moment of truth."

When you need it most, someone is going to *trust what you say*, and by default, they are going *to trust you*!

They are going to *know* that you are telling the truth!

And someday, you might even need to use the "atom bomb" of "rectal candor" on someone either for your own benefit or theirs—and it will only detonate *if your own reputation is sound*.

Think you can be a *great* manager without the reputation of being a truth teller?

Think you can be a great person without that reputation?

I bet if I were to ask you, you could easily name off the top of your head the people in your life you know to be truth tellers and who are pretty consistent liars.

Question?

If you ask that about yourself—which list would *you* be on?

1.61 Love

Now, some of you might be a little disgruntled with me for leaving this topic until the end, but it's the most important difference between a "great manager" and a "bad" or even "good" one.

Love?

Yes.

Here's how I frame it within the work environment:

Drum roll…

This is it!

Ready?

In order to be a great manager it is not necessary for you to *like* the people that work for you—*but*—*you must love them*!

Love?

What the heck does "love" have to do with being a great manager?

Ugh!

Answer:

Everything!

First—in my defense—let me say this:

I don't really like "people" very much to begin with. I mean, in a broad general sense.

They mostly annoy me.

This "problem with people" started almost as early as I can remember:

Kindergarten? The kid that wouldn't just lie down and quietly take his/her friggin' nap?

Those kids in my "gifted" class? Ugh!

Inconsiderate drivers?

People in front of me at the grocery store who don't know how to use their credit card or spend 15 minutes digging for change?

Rude people?

Obnoxious people?

Guys who think they're "smart" but don't have their own Gulfstream?

Dumb-ass people?

Cheap people? Don't get me started!

Anyway:

I'm just saying that "love" of my fellow humans isn't something that is a "natural" part of my wheelhouse.

Just like happiness, I had to work on it.

In fact, I'm still working on it.

On the other hand:

My wife?

Love beyond measure.

My friends?

Yes!

My dog if I had one?

Yes!

My staff?

Love.

As I mentioned, I might not exactly "like" everyone who works for me, but once they are on my "team," *they are on my team*!

Love.

Love?

What do you mean you "love" your staff?

Answer:

To the extent that is reasonable, I fight for their pay.

I fight for their benefits.

I fight for their schedules.

I fight for their safety.

I fight to give them the tools they need to do their job.

I fight to make sure they are being treated with respect.

I tell them what I can do for them and what I cannot.

Most importantly—I tell them the truth.

Guess what?

They know it!

They are on *my* team!

How do they know it?

Because they have seen me consistently demonstrate all of the above on countless occasions and because I have been very consistent about:

Treating them like human beings!

Does that mean they think I'm a pushover?

Hardly. They know I'd fire my mother if she weren't doing the job, God rest her soul.

Do they trust me?

Yes. Even if they won't admit it.

Will they turn on me in a minute if they don't get their way?

Yes. They're human.

Do I hold that against them?

No. They're human.

Is what I do for them ever "enough"?

No.

And, most of the time, they're probably right.

"Well," you say, "you can't talk about love in a professional environment. You can't talk about 'love' being a critical component of great management. It's just goofy."

Okay.

Then let me ask you this:

Would you follow someone into "hell and back" that you didn't love?

Would they follow you?

Here's my point and I'll let this go:

If you—as a manager—are incapable of "loving" your staff, you will never be a "great" manager.

You might be able to be "good."

But…

You will never be "great."

Here's why:

Because, unless you love them, *they will not love you.*

And…

If they do not love you, then they will never work for you because *they want to* but only because they *have to*—so *they* will never be great.

Big difference?

I think so—and I think you do too.

By the way, "saying" that you love anything is way different than "acting" like it.

Actions speak much louder.

Remember at the outset of this book we asked this question:

How do I get these people to do what I want them to do *because they want to do it?*

Love.

Much more importantly:

How do I get them to want to *do it for me?*

Love.

1.62 If It's Not Fun

I once had the delightful experience of working with a woman by the name of Deborah Rivers. She was my Director of Sales and Marketing at a small but posh hotel in Portland, but her background prior to working with me was with Ritz Carlton.

I remember Deb recounting her experience at a Ritz sales and marketing meeting she had attended earlier in her career where the speaker had opened the meeting with the following profound words:

"If it's not fun, fuck it!"

Exactly!

Now, I have no idea what that speaker went on to say in that meeting—but whatever it was—he was right on the money with his opening statement.

I've met a lot of people in my career who seem hell bent on just the opposite. They're the "glass half empty" folks I talked about earlier that focus on all of the things "wrong" in life and at work.

Nothing, it seems, can be said or done to dissuade them from their own misery.

They are *not* having fun.

I know these people well.

A very long time ago, I used to be one of them.

Then, one day many years ago, when I was on one of my usual rants, discussing all that was wrong in the world with one of my friends, he said this:

"Sometimes in order to be happy—you have to be prepared to fight for it. Are you prepared to fight for it?"

Rectal candor!

And in this case, by "fight" my friend really meant, "change."

In this case, "prepared" meant, "brave."

Perhaps:

Brave enough to change the job you don't like.

Brave enough to change the relationship you don't like.

Brave enough to stop allowing yourself to be bullied.

Brave enough to focus on what you *do* have as opposed to what you *don't.*

Brave enough to go to work—*to do something!*

Brave enough to stop "moaning."

Brave enough to stop thinking "shit."

Brave enough to tell the truth.

As I have aged, my time and the way I spend it has become progressively more important to me.

I'm not a big believer in the "afterlife," so how I live in this one is paramount.

Maybe I'm wrong. Maybe there is eternal bliss. We'll see.

In the meantime, there is no reason not to enjoy this life while I'm waiting around to see what happens afterwards.

In the meantime, I know about "now."

And "now," while I'm still breathing, I'd like to have fun:

I'd like to love what I do professionally.

I'd like to love the people I hang around.

I'd like to love what I do privately.

Especially:

I'd like to not spend one second worried about things beyond my control.

And...

I generally don't.

I've gotten pretty good at *insisting* on happiness.

In fact, if push comes to shove, I'm even prepared to "fight" for it if necessary.

Indeed, Ritz Carlton sales and marketing speaker of many years ago:

"If it's not fun, fuck it!"

Words to live by.

PS—in the process of writing this book, Deb told me that she recalled that particular speaker was Wally Amos, the founder of the Famous Amos Cookie Company. Credit where credit is due!

1.OH Christmas Story

I'd like to end my little rant with a Christmas story.

Really, it's more of a management story that just happened to occur many years ago during the Christmas season.

First some background:

I was probably in my second year as a catering director at one of the company's busiest hotels in San Jose, California. Now, this was in the late '80s when Silicon Valley was still "becoming" Silicon Valley and just beginning its charge.

The hotel was still relatively new and one of the few that could do large catering events, so the holiday season was always crazy busy. With the meeting space totally booked, we could serve approximately 3,000 guests at one time. Now, there are a lot of hotels much bigger that can serve a lot more—but we thought at the time that serving 3,000 covers was a massive undertaking.

Those of us that worked there jokingly liked to refer to the hotel as the "steam-roller." Either you were "on it" or "under it." When I had been first promoted to the property, I had spent a good portion of my time "under it." I was still young and beautiful and hadn't really figured out "anything" yet regarding management.

As an example, I still remember showing up for work one morning only to discover about 600 people in one of the meeting room foyers waiting for the doors to open for a breakfast meeting. The only problem was: no one at the hotel, including me, knew anything about it!

The banquet event order had been "misplaced."

No banquet crew had been scheduled.

The chef had no idea about it, etc.

But the meeting planner had *his* copy of the BEO, which he was happy to show me. He was so pissed off—and rightfully so—I thought he was going to kill me!

Anyhow, we somehow pulled that breakfast off, but not without the meeting planner hating me, the chef hating me, and a good part of the entire hotel staff hating me including the GM.

Live and learn.

Fast-forward two years and back to my "Christmas" story:

It was the last Saturday night before Christmas Day proper—really the "end" of holiday season parties at the hotel—and

I knew when I woke up that morning that the day was going to be crazy. We had a few big holiday breakfasts booked, then lunch was maxed out, and the dinner parties would be packed in like sardines.

I got up and went surfing with a friend of mine in Santa Cruz, so by the time I showed up in the office it was already 9am or so.

Why, on such a busy day, would I go surfing?

Because I had, by this time, "total" faith in my staff. And, I had also learned that there are only so many days in life that you get to go surfing. And, I had learned that my staff needed to do some things on their own.

Despite my faith, when I finally rolled in to the catering office, I half expected to hear that "something" had happened or gone wrong with the morning breakfasts.

Nope. Apparently not.

There was an almost eerie calm in the office. I had one administrative assistant, four catering coordinators and an assistant catering director. They were all at their desks working away, smiling and laughing about how well the day was going so far. Their desks were neat as pins, their nametags shiny.

I reached up to make sure I had my nametag on—it was one of my "things" and they knew it.

I went to my office and picked up my list of all the events for the day. We called it a catering "package," which had been "invented" not long after we'd missed that big breakfast and a multitude of other details concerning other events.

My "package" had a cover sheet, which was basically a 24hr "map" of the hotel banquet space, with each function listed, including number of attendees, type of event, and times. This was followed with copies all of the pertinent BEOs for the day, which had been double checked the day before by the coordinators, checked again by the PM banquet manager the night before, who also checked with the kitchen to make sure they had everything we had, then checked again that morning by the opening banquet captain or manager, and double checked once more with the Chef.

The BEOs themselves had all of the event details, the menus, and the final count of attendees. The BEOs also listed the banquet staff scheduled to work by name and time.

In short, I had all of the details of every event in my hand, including exactly who was working and when, so I didn't need to ask my staff any questions—particularly ones they would regard as "stupid."

As I headed to the back to MBWA, I asked my assistant catering director again:

"So, everything is going okay so far?"

"Yes, boss. The breakfasts are almost done. They're getting ready for the big flips to lunch. I'm going back in a minute."

Reassured, I took my precious banquet "package" and headed to the banquet corridor.

Now, I have to tell you, I have never seen a hotel with a better banquet layout than the one I worked at in San Jose. When I entered the service corridor, I could look straight down it to the very end of the first floor, past the kitchen, the purchasing area, and the employee cafeteria. All of the banquet rooms were accessed directly from this one massive hallway, with a similar one on the second floor to access a large ballroom there.

Kudos to the architects, it was a brilliant design!

At the very end of the service corridor, we had converted one of the banquet storage areas to a banquet office. Just outside of it, we had installed a flag holder.

Now, depending on how the day was going, certain flags were displayed:

Green meant the day was going great.

Yellow meant we'd had some problems or hiccups but they'd been solved.

Red meant we were having some big problems.

Black, complete with skull and crossbones, meant the day was totally in the shit and couldn't be salvaged.

And...

My favorite...

The American flag, which meant that the day was awesome!

Any one of my captains and or my assistant catering director were free to change the flags given the "conditions of the moment," but I reserved the right to be the only one who could raise the American flag.

Now, you might think it was goofy, but my staff *loved* the flags. And, if and when the flag went from green to yellow or even to red, they took great joy in attempting to get the flag back to green.

So, when I opened the door to that corridor, you might imagine that the first thing I looked for was the banquet flag, which to my delight was waving green at the far end of the starkly lit corridor.

I worked my way to the kitchen and spoke to the Chef. He was happy. My banquet captains had been all over him with counts and timing.

I spoke to my staff, but didn't offer any input if asked about specific operational issues.

"What did your captain say?" I would ask in response, purposely avoiding giving them an answer I was not supposed to give.

Anyway, the day progressed and was typically crazy.

After a busy breakfast, we had 3,000 people eat lunch and leave, and then cleaned and turned the banquet rooms and set for 3,000 more for dinner and dancing. Housekeepers were doubling as banquet servers and were hastily fit with banquet uniforms. We were so busy my banquet manager had even recruited some of the maintenance crew and landscapers as well. The Chef had recruited anyone left including me to man his massive "dish-up" lines.

In the meantime, I wandered around, rolling rounds and setting tables, careful to avoid giving any input.

"Boss, where do you want…?"

"Where did your captain say to put it?"

"Boss, what time do you…?"

"What time did your captain say?"

Later, after the last meals were being cleared, I did my best to *personally* thank everyone who had worked, particularly those from other departments. I stopped by each of the banquet rooms and then made my way to the kitchen to thank the Chef and his staff.

Here's the thing:

I had made it a point all evening to "do nothing."

I let my staff do everything!

Sure, I set tables and helped physically, carrying trays of food and clearing tables, but I hadn't really done *anything* "managerially."

And…

My staff knew it.

And…

They were proud of it.

And…

I *loved* them for it.

And…

They knew it.

And...

I went to the banquet office, found that American flag, and hung it in the corridor so that my staff—many of whom who had just pulled 12 to 16 hour shifts *for me*—would see it on their way out the door.

We had just set the record for the one-day catering revenue in the hotel, the best December revenue ever, and we had crushed the previous year by more than 10%!

Really, it hadn't been me at all who had done it.

Really, it had been *my staff*!

I remember leaving the hotel that night and having an epiphany:

So that's how it's supposed to work.

Oh!

Dedication

I'd like to dedicate this book to one of the most oddly inspirational guys I have ever worked for. He was a man by the name of Chuck Indermuehle.

Chuck was kind of a scary looking guy, who basically reminded me of well-fed German SS officer with a bad attitude like you sometimes see in the movies. In fact, if he had gone to Hollywood instead of getting stuck in the hospitality business, I'm sure Chuck could have done quite well cast in those types of roles if he could have mastered a German accent and otherwise just pretty much been himself.

I knew him for years, first as a regional VP for a former hotel company we both worked for, then again when he was gracious enough to give me a general manager job at another company he had gone to work for later.

One time, when I was still a little "wet-behind-the-ears," Chuck was sitting across my desk, and we were discussing some employee or some problem that had been caused by one.

Well, I think ole Chuck must have thought my proposed remedy for the situation was a little "soft," because he leaned forward, narrowed his eyes like he was about to kill me, and uttered these words:

"You know what your problem is, Frazier? You haven't learned to hate people yet!"

Then, he sat back and laughed, sort of like the alien in Predator. Deep long and loud, it was truly a wonderful laugh.

Obviously, Chuck had been kidding, but I was a little slow to catch on.

I still think about that day often and fondly. It was one of those "moments" in your career that stand out. One of those moments that seem oddly profound.

I stayed in touch with Chuck long after he had retired. I liked to call him on the phone occasionally and "pose" as a disgruntled IRS agent that was about to audit his taxes. I think he got a big kick out of it.

Now, in retrospect, what I might have told Chuck when he was still alive—or really only whispered down a well—is this:

"No Chuck. In fact, it's quite the opposite. My problem—my life-long struggle—has been learning to love them."

About Me

I have been in the hospitality business for over 45 years, beginning with my first "real" job at the tender age of 16 as a sous chef at a steak house in Redding, California. My starting wage was $1.65 per hour. It's hard to imagine now that such a wage ever existed, or more importantly, where the time went.

Over the course of my career, I have worked in three-star, four-star and five-star hotels in various positions, along with work at the corporate level for two hotel companies.

Some of my past jobs have included: paperboy, logger/choke setter, dishwasher, busboy, waiter, line cook, kitchen manager, butler, banquet manager, catering director, food and beverage director, assistant hotel general manager, corporate catering director, restaurant manager, hotel general manager, and VP of hotel operations.

One of my most memorable jobs was in college, where every Saturday, I would fry up a weeks' worth of tortilla chips for the Mexican Restaurant I worked at as a server the rest of the week. Often, I was very hung-over and the kitchen was not air-conditioned, so you can imagine. The temperature during the summer was often well over 100 degrees. But someone had to fry the chips—damn it! And, it did give me lots of time to ponder the meaning of life as the hot steam and grease evaporated into the scalding air around me.

As mentioned in the book, I also hold Bachelor of Arts degrees in English Literature and Philosophy. I blame my extreme interest in religion for pursuing both degrees and for the resulting permanent religious skepticism I acquired in the process.

I have been fortunate enough to live in Hawaii for the past 20 years with my beautiful wife Jolanta and a large freshwater aquarium full of unnamed fish. I don't have a dog right now, but I plan to get one when I am ready to completely upset my otherwise semi-peaceful life.

My current hobbies include; surfing, ocean swimming, motorcycling, travel, and cleaning things. I have in the past also been proficient at skydiving, scuba diving, snow skiing, water skiing, and horseback riding. One time I even flew a fighter jet! Yes, the pilot actually let me fly it! I love to go fast, I'll say that. Thanks Skip!

In addition to Management-One-Point-Oh, I have also authored two science fiction novels, titled In Situ and In Natura, which are available on Amazon. Please buy them! I'm no Hemingway, but they're fun reads if I do say so myself.

For more information, visit me at davidsamuelfrazier.com.

Appendix/References

MIAMI VICE—my reference comes from an episode called Definitely Miami 2.12

ROGER DAWSON—some of my negotiation remarks are from his brilliant "Secrets of Power Negotiating." Highly recommended!

ONE MINUTE MANAGER—my reference to MBWA and other management tactics come from my early exposure to this excellent book by Kenneth Blanchard and Spencer Johnson.

VIKTOR FRANKL—recommended reading if you want to find out what a "tough life" really looks like, particularly his masterpiece "Man's Search for Meaning."

THE BIG CHILL—1983 movie written by Lawrence Kasdan and Barbara Benedek.

QUOTES—all of my quotations are credited in the body or are so common I didn't bother to name the "originator" since no one apparently knows who that was.

FISH TACOS

Here's the longer example I invented to describe a "false analogy" or "false comparison."

I call it "Fish Tacos":

A restaurant ownership group has 3 Fish Taco restaurants that are nearly identical. They all seat 20 customers and they all serve about 80 people per day. The ownership group likes these restaurants because they are small, fairly easy to operate and easy to understand—particularly since *all three restaurants are so similar.*

Now, the owners have a manager—let's call him Dave. The owners like Dave. He has operated all 3 restaurants for several years, almost always beating the very conservative budgets that the owners typically establish. They set the budgets and operate under the 5/3/5 formula: that is, 5% increase in revenue per year, no more than a 3% increase in labor, and of course, a 5% increase in net profit.)

Keep it simple.

So far—so good.

Dave has done a good job and almost always beats the annual revenue increase goal by a couple of points. For example, this year Dave has raised the average check almost 7% so that it's now about $10 for a fish taco plate.

However, at the start of the year, 4 local groups approached Dave about hosting their daily meetings at *one* of his Fish Taco restaurants—maybe the Denny's shut down, who knows? But, since the restaurant was so small, Dave realized that in order to accommodate the groups, the restaurant would essentially have to be "shut down" and *only serve the new groups.*

Anyway, Dave did some quick math on the back of a napkin and determined that he would need to charge the groups the following in order to risk shutting down the restaurant to regular customers:

The first 3 groups of 20 would have to pay $15 per person (i.e., a $5 premium) and the last group of only 10 people would have to pay $20 per person. They agreed.

Here is what happened:

Restaurants #1 and #2 continued to gross $800 per day (i.e., 80 covers at $10). Labor for his one hostess and one server cost $100 for both, netting a "front of the house" profit of $700 and a labor percentage of 12%.

Rest #3—the "group" restaurant—began to gross $1,100 dollars per day (i.e., 60 covers at $15 and 10 covers at $20). However, in order to properly service the groups, Dave had to add an additional hostess/cashier and one additional server for a total front-of-house labor cost of $200 per day. Even so, this resulted in a front-of-house profit of $900!

In short, by taking the groups at the higher average checks, Dave had significantly increased the FOH profit of restaurant #3 over the other two restaurants, with even less cost in the kitchen, etc., due to the "predictability" of the group business.

Dave, of course, was very proud of himself.

That is, until the annual ownership meeting.

Here were the owner's rather unhappy questions:

Why is the front-of-house labor so "high" at restaurant #3?

Why is the average check so "low" at restaurants #1 and #2?

Lesson:

Don't get confused by letting others pretend you are comparing "apples with apples" when you are really comparing "apples with oranges."

Clearly, restaurant #3 is now kicking ass in terms of overall profit, but the owners, used to years of certain statistics, might even be confused themselves about what might be best for their business.

And, even though Dave had increased the annual FOH profit in restaurant #3 by $73,000, the owners might still have a problem with the labor increases or not understand why Dave can't also get the average check to $15.70 in *all* the restaurants!

Seems crazy?

I've been there. Not in this specific scenario, but very similar ones.

Here's the point:

YOU need to be able to recognize that it's a false comparison and the reasons why!

And maybe, in that sort of situation, if you cannot win that argument—for the sake of everyone's sanity—your best move might be to "fire" the "groups" and go back to the same-ole-same-ole in order to give the owner's *what they want.*

In my example, they may simply want more congruency in their operations. Period.

And, *that is their prerogative!*

Remember—at work—who your most important customer is?

Yes, *the boss or bosses!*

Sometimes, in my experience, it's better to pick your battles.

"My mind is made up. Don't confuse me with the facts."

Impossible to beat that one…

Surrender.

But…

Make sure if you are doing comparisons that they are legitimate ones.

More importantly:

Make sure no one is pulling a "false comparison" on you!

Made in the
USA
Middletown, DE